# Poems for Comparison and Contrast

# Poems for Comparison and Contrast

Robert J. Conley
*Southwest Missouri State College*

Richard L. Cherry
*University of Illinois*

The Macmillan Company, New York

THE MACMILLAN COMPANY
866 THIRD AVENUE, NEW YORK, NEW YORK 10022

COLLIER-MACMILLAN CANADA, LTD., TORONTO, ONTARIO

Library of Congress catalog card number: 78–156985

First Printing

## *Credits and Acknowledgments*

Copyrighted works, listed in the order of appearance, are reprinted in the United States, its possessions and dependencies, the Philippines, and Canada, by permission of the following:

"Come, Live with Me and Be My Love" by C. Day Lewis, one of *Two Songs* taken from COLLECTED POEMS 1954. Copyright 1954 by C. Day Lewis, reprinted by permission of the Harold Matson Company, Inc., the Hogarth Press, and Jonathan Cape Ltd.

"Not Marble nor the Gilded Monuments" and "The End of the World" by Archibald MacLeish, from COLLECTED POEMS 1917–1952. Copyright, 1952, by Archibald MacLeish. Reprinted by permission of the publisher, Houghton Mifflin Company.

"Elegy for Jane." Copyright 1950 by Theodore Roethke from COLLECTED POEMS OF THEODORE ROETHKE. Reprinted by permission of Doubleday & Company, Inc.

"To Anne Herrick, in Heaven" by Dean Deter, 1969, reprinted by permission of The Black Bull Press and Dean Deter, from POEMS FROM SLEEPLESS SUMMER NIGHTS: 1967–1969. "A Letter to One of the Pre-historic Indians Who Built the Mounds at Circleville, Ohio" by Dean Deter. Reprinted by permission of Dean Deter.

"Counting the Beats" by Robert Graves. Reprinted by permission of Collins-Knowlton-Wing, Inc. Copyright © 1961 Robert Graves.

"The Clearing" by LeRoi Jones, from PREFACE TO A TWENTY VOLUME SUICIDE NOTE. Copyright © 1961 by LeRoi Jones. Reprinted by permission of Corinth Books.

"Shelley's Skylark" and "The Darkling Thrush" by Thomas Hardy. Reprinted with permission of The Macmillan Company from COLLECTED POEMS by Thomas Hardy. Copyright 1925 by The Macmillan Company, the Trustees of The Hardy Estate, and Macmillan & Company Ltd. "Waiting Both" by Thomas Hardy. Reprinted with permission of The Macmillan Company from COLLECTED POEMS by Thomas Hardy. Copyright 1925 by The Macmillan Company, renewed 1953 by Lloyds Bank, Ltd.

"A Thrush Before Dawn" by Alice Meynell from ALICE MEYNELL: PROSE

v

# *Preface*

*Poems for Comparison and Contrast* is designed primarily for the beginning student of poetry. We feel that the main task of such a book is not simply to teach technical poetic components, but to provide through a careful selection of poems a means for the student to develop a sensitivity to the broader effects of poetry. The basic assumption of this book is the important and widely held theory that in the final analysis the form and content of a poem cannot be separated, that the poem's *meaning* is utterly dependent on the *how* of its composition—that, indeed, a poem *is* what it *does*.

There is a popular misconception about the nature of poetry which holds that a really good poem does not say what it means directly, that the *real* meaning of the poem is hidden away somewhere beneath layers of irony, various forms of symbolism, and other complex literary gimmickry; and that, therefore, it takes a very special and highly analytic mind to get at that meaning. One negative result of this misconception is that poetry all too often is regarded by the student from an attitude of defeat even before he has attacked it. He is apt to feel that the best he can possibly do is patiently to await "the word" from the front of the room that will give him the secret of the meaning of the poem and to accept that word without hesitation or question, without even beginning to hope for any kind of real understanding. This misconception is partly a result of beginning discussions of poetry with lists of terms and with lofty generalizations about the nature of poetry.

With that in mind, this book is organized to facilitate beginning at the primary source—that is, with a poem. It then proceeds to another poem, which for some reason or other is similar to the first one. Now, it is not at all a difficult matter for any person who can reason to notice the similarities of two poems just from reading them, and he does not need to feel at home with the professional jargon of poets and teachers of poetry to comment on them. It is a relatively small step from this point to comments on the differences between the two poems, and we believe that the simple recognition of these points of comparison and contrast leads to a rapid understanding of the nature of poetry itself. If the instructor is concerned with the terminology of poetry, he can easily supply it when the discussion itself seems to call for it. The whole point of this approach is that we do not begin with a preconceived method of feeding poems to students, but rather allow the *students*, through observation and discussion, to discover the method.

We have placed the poems, therefore, in large thematic units and within each unit have juxtaposed each poem with another or, in some cases, with two or three other poems primarily on the following bases:

*Theme:* Wordsworth's "Mutability" with Shelley's "Mutability"; Marvell's "To His Coy Mistress" with Herrick's "To the Virgins, to Make Much of Time."

*Imagery:* Herrick's "To Daffodils" with Wordsworth's "I Wandered Lonely as a Cloud."

*Metaphor:* Raleigh's "What Is Our Life?" with Shakespeare's "All the World's a Stage" and Poe's "The Conqueror Worm."

*Tone:* Shakespeare's "Sonnet CXXX" with MacLeish's "Not Marble nor the Gilded Monuments."

*Symbol:* Whitman's "To a Locomotive in Winter" with Dickinson's "I Like to See It Lap the Miles."

The bases of comparison listed above provide only a beginning. For example, it is possible to proceed from the observation that Whitman and Dickinson are both writing about trains, and both using the trains in a symbolic way, to a discussion of the imagery in the two poems, which is quite different. Other things, such as meter and tone, again quite different here, can then be examined. At the end of the discussion, some idea should have been formed of the nature of those elements in each poem that make it something unique in spite of its similarities to the other in the pair. In other words, we feel that this juxtaposition can become a dramatic illustration of the earlier statement—that the *meaning* of the poem is utterly dependent on the *how* of its composition.

In selecting the poems, we have taken into consideration the need for adequate representation of the major poets of the various periods of English and American poetry.

We have included as an appendix to the text William K. Wimsatt's excellent and very useful essay, "What to Say About a Poem." This essay points out what should be the major concerns of a critical reader in order to arrive at how and why a poem "means." Further study and analysis of the poems themselves, using the principles outlined by Wimsatt, will enable the student to arrive at an initial understanding of how a poem works.

R. J. C.
R. L. C.

# Contents

## Section II

## Section III

## Section IV

## Section V

## Section VI

# Section VII

# Section VIII

# Section IX

# Section X

# Appendix

# Index

# Section I

CHRISTOPHER MARLOWE
## The Passionate Shepherd to His Love

Come live with me and be my love,
And we will all the pleasures prove
That valleys, groves, hills, and fields,
Woods, or steepy mountain yields.

5 And we will sit upon the rocks,
Seeing the shepherds feed their flocks,
By shallow rivers to whose falls
Melodious birds sing madrigals.

And I will make thee beds of roses
10 And a thousand fragrant posies,
A cap of flowers, and a kirtle°                    Dress
Embroidered all with leaves of myrtle;

A gown made of the finest wool
Which from our pretty lambs we pull;
15 Fair lined slippers for the cold,
With buckles of the purest gold;

A belt of straw and ivy buds,
With coral clasps and amber studs:
And if these pleasures may thee move,
20 Come live with me, and be my love.

The shepherds' swains shall dance and sing
For thy delight each May morning:
If these delights thy mind may move,
Then live with me and be my love.


SIR WALTER RALEIGH
## The Nymph's Reply to the Shepherd

If all the world and love were young,
And truth in every shepherd's tongue,
These pretty pleasures might me move
To live with thee and be thy love.

5   Time drives the flocks from field to fold
     When rivers rage and rocks grow cold,
     And Philomel° becometh dumb;            *Nightingale*
     The rest complains of cares to come.

     The flowers do fade, and wanton fields
10   To wayward winter reckoning yields;
     A honey tongue, a heart of gall,
     Is fancy's spring, but sorrow's fall.

     Thy gowns, thy shoes, thy beds of roses,
     Thy cap, thy kirtle, and thy posies
15   Soon break, soon wither, soon forgotten—
     In folly ripe, in reason rotten.

     Thy belt of straw and ivy buds,
     Thy coral clasps and amber studs,
     All these in me no means can move
20   To come to thee and be thy love.

     But could youth last and love still breed,
     Had joys no date nor age no need,
     Then these delights my mind might move
     To live with thee and be thy love.

## JOHN DONNE
### The Bait

     Come live with me, and be my love,
     And we will some new pleasures prove,
     Of golden sands, and crystal brooks,
     With silken lines, and silver hooks.

5   There will the river whispering run,
     Warmed by thy eyes more than the sun.
     And there th' enamoured fish will stay,
     Begging° themselves they may betray.         *Begging that*

     When thou wilt swim in that live bath,
10   Each fish, which every channel hath,
     Will amorously to thee swim,
     Gladder to catch thee, than thou him.

If thou, to be so seen, beest loath,
By sun or moon, thou dark'nest both;
15    And if myself have leave to see,
I need not their light, having thee.

Let others freeze with angling reeds,°          *Rods*
And cut their legs with shells and weeds,
Or treacherously poor fish beset
20    With strangling snare, or windowy net.

Let coarse bold hands from slimy nest
The bedded fish in banks out-wrest,
Or curious traitors, sleave-silk° flies,      *Silk thread*
Bewitch poor fishes' wandering eyes.

25    For thee, thou need'st no such deceit,
For thou thyself art thine own bait;
That fish that is not catched thereby,
Alas, is wiser far than I.

# C. DAY LEWIS
## *Come, Live with Me and Be My Love*

Come, live with me and be my love,
And we will all the pleasures prove
Of peace and plenty, bed and board,
That chance employment may afford.

5    I'll handle dainties on the docks
And thou shalt read of summer frocks:
At evening by the sour canals
We'll hope to hear some madrigals.

Care on thy maiden brow shall put
10    A wreath of wrinkles, and thy foot
Be shod with pain: not silken dress
But toil shall tire thy loveliness.

Hunger shall make thy modest zone
And cheat fond death of all but bone—
15    If these delights thy mind may move,
Then live with me and be my love.

THOMAS LOVELL BEDDOES
*Song*

   How many times do I love thee, dear?
     Tell me how many thoughts there be
       In the atmosphere
       Of a new-fall'n year,
5  Whose white and sable hours appear
     The latest flake of Eternity:—
   So many times do I love thee, dear.

   How many times do I love again?
     Tell me how many beads there are
10      In a silver chain
       Of evening rain,
  Unravelled from the tumbling main,
     And threading the eye of a yellow star:—
   So many times do I love again.

ELIZABETH BARRETT BROWNING
*How Do I Love Thee?*
*From* Sonnets from the Portuguese

### XLIII

  How do I love thee? Let me count the ways.
  I love thee to the depth and breadth and height
  My soul can reach, when feeling out of sight
  For the ends of Being and ideal Grace.
5  I love thee to the level of every day's
  Most quiet need, by sun and candlelight.
  I love thee freely, as men strive for Right;
  I love thee purely, as they turn from Praise;
  I love thee with the passion put to use
10  In my old griefs, and with my childhood's faith.
  I love thee with a love I seemed to lose
  With my lost saints,—I love thee with the breath
  Smiles, tears, of all my life!—and, if God choose,
  I shall but love thee better after death.

# ANDREW MARVELL
## *To His Coy Mistress*

Had we but world enough, and time,
This coyness, lady, were no crime.
We would sit down, and think which way
To walk, and pass our long love's day.
5  Thou by the Indian Ganges' side
Shouldst rubies° find; I by the tide
Of Humber would complain. I would
Love you ten years before the flood,
And you should, if you please, refuse
10  Till the conversion of the Jews.
My vegetable° love should grow
Vaster than empires and more slow;
An hundred years should go to praise
Thine eyes, and on thy forehead gaze;
15  Two hundred to adore each breast,
But thirty thousand to the rest;
An age at least to every part,
And the last age should show your heart.
For, lady, you deserve this state,
20  Nor would I love at lower rate.
    But at my back I always hear
Time's wingéd chariot hurrying near;
And yonder all before us lie
Deserts of vast eternity.
25  Thy beauty shall no more be found;
Nor, in thy marble vault, shall sound
My echoing song; then worms shall try
That long-preserved virginity,
And your quaint honor turn to dust,
30  And into ashes all my lust:
The grave's a fine and private place,
But none, I think, do there embrace.
    Now therefore, while the youthful hue
Sits on thy skin like morning glow,
35  And while thy willing soul transpires
At every pore with instant fires,
Now let us sport us while we may,
And now, like amorous birds of prey,
Rather at once our time devour
40  Than languish in his slow-chapped power.

*Talismans for the
preservation of
virginity*

*Flourishing without
conscious nurture*

7

Let us roll all our strength and all
Our sweetness up into one ball,
And tear our pleasures with rough strife
Thorough the iron gates of life:
45 Thus, though we cannot make our sun
Stand still, yet we will make him run.


ROBERT HERRICK
*To the Virgins, to Make Much of Time*

Gather ye rosebuds while ye may,
 Old time is still a-flying;
And this same flower that smiles today
 Tomorrow will be dying.

5 The glorious lamp of heaven, the sun,
 The higher he's a-getting,
The sooner will his race be run,
 And nearer he's to setting.

That age is best which is the first,
10 When youth and blood are warmer;
But being spent, the worse, and worst
 Times still succeed the former.

Then be not coy, but use your time,
 And, while ye may, go marry;
15 For, having lost but once your prime,
 You may forever tarry.

MICHAEL DRAYTON
*Since There's No Help*
*From* Idea

### Sonnet LXI

Since there's no help, come let us kiss and part;
Nay, I have done, you get no more of me,
And I am glad, yea glad with all my heart

That thus so cleanly I myself can free;
5  Shake hands forever, cancel all our vows,
And when we meet at any time again,
Be it not seen in either of our brows
That we one jot of former love retain.
Now at the last gasp of love's latest breath,
10 When, his pulse failing, passion speechless lies,
When faith is kneeling by his bed of death,
And innocence is closing up his eyes,
    Now if thou wouldst, when all have given him over,
    From death to life thou mightst him yet recover.


SIR JOHN SUCKLING
*Song*

    Why so pale and wan, fond lover?
        Prithee, why so pale?
    Will, when looking well can't move her,
        Looking ill prevail?
5       Prithee, why so pale?

    Why so dull and mute, young sinner?
        Prithee, why so mute?
    Will, when speaking well can't win her,
        Saying nothing do 't?
10      Prithee, why so mute?

    Quit, quit, for shame; this will not move,
        This cannot take her.
    If of herself she will not love,
        Nothing can make her:
15      The devil take her!

WILLIAM SHAKESPEARE
*My Mistress' Eyes Are Nothing Like the Sun*

CXXX

My mistress' eyes are nothing like the sun;
Coral is far more red than her lips' red;

9

If snow be white, why then her breasts are dun;
If hairs be wires, black wires grow on her head.
5   I have seen roses damasked,° red and white,                    *Variegated*
But no such roses see I in her cheeks;
And in some perfumes is there more delight
Than in the breath that from my mistress reeks.
I love to hear her speak, yet well I know
10  That music hath a far more pleasing sound;
I grant I never saw a goddess go;°                              *Walk*
My mistress, when she walks, treads on the ground.
And yet, by heaven, I think my love as rare
As any she belied with false compare.


## ARCHIBALD MACLEISH
### *Not Marble nor the Gilded Monuments*

The praisers of women in their proud and beautiful poems
Naming the grave mouth and the hair and the eyes
Boasted those they loved should be forever remembered
These were lies

5   The words sound but the face in the Istrian° sun is forgotten
The poet speaks but to her dead ears no more
The sleek throat is gone—and the breast that was troubled to
      listen
Shadow from door

Therefore I will not praise your knees nor your fine walking
10  Telling you men shall remember your name as long
As lips move or breath is spent or the iron of English
Rings from a tongue

I shall say you were young and your arms straight and your
      mouth scarlet
I shall say you will die and none will remember you
15  Your arms change and none remember the swish of your
      garments
Nor the click of your shoe

Not with my hand's strength not with difficult labor
Springing the obstinate words to the bones of your breast

° A peninsula in Italy and Yugoslavia, extending into the Adriatic.

And the stubborn line to your young stride and the breath to
    your breathing
20  And the beat to your haste
Shall I prevail on the hearts of unborn men to remember

(What is a dead girl but a shadowy ghost
Or a dead man's voice but a distant and vain affirmation
Like dream words most)

25  Therefore I will not speak of the undying glory of women
I will say you were young and straight and your skin fair
And you stood in the door and the sun was a shadow of leaves
    on your shoulders
And a leaf on your hair

I will not speak of the famous beauty of dead women
30  I will say the shape of a leaf lay once on your hair
Till the world ends and the eyes are out and the mouths broken
Look! It is there!

## THEODORE ROETHKE
*Elegy for Jane*
My Student, Thrown by a Horse

I remember the neckcurls, limp and damp as tendrils;
And her quick look, a sidelong pickerel smile;
And how, once startled into talk, the light syllables leaped for
    her,
And she balanced in the delight of her thought,
5  A wren, happy, tail into the wind,
Her song trembling the twigs and small branches.
The shade sang with her;
The leaves, their whispers turned to kissing;
And the mold sang in the bleached valleys under the rose.

10  Oh, when she was sad, she cast herself down into such a pure
    depth,
Even a father could not find her:
Scraping her cheek against straw;
Stirring the clearest water.

My sparrow, you are not here,
15   Waiting like a fern, making a spiny shadow.
The sides of wet stones cannot console me,
Nor the moss, wound with the last light.

If only I could nudge you from this sleep,
My maimed darling, my skittery pigeon.
20   Over this damp grave I speak the words of my love:
I, with no rights in this matter,
Neither father nor lover.


## DEAN DETER
### *To Anne Herrick, in Heaven*

Anne Herrick stands immobile now,
cast in stone, at the far other end
of life's mortality.
Her stern skirts never rustle
5   with the wind that moves
stars closer to the world's edge.

Young skin against young skin,
lovers nervously nestle in amongst
the graves, hurrying to do
10   what they've almost done so many times.

And what will you tell them, Anne,
this night? Will you mention your young
man, now also dead, and the night you first
came to this graveyard?

15   What stone guards the mound,
holding thighs forever shut
that once sighed apart with your love?

Anne, hold out your hands;
there will be time, soon enough,
20   to talk.
Let them reach into each other
and draw out a bone to break
and place at your feet.

What penance will you require
25   for disturbing your sleep?
There will be time, Anne;
it grows late,
and you must sleep.

JOHN DONNE
*The Canonization*

For God's sake hold your tongue, and let me love,
    Or chide my palsy, or my gout,
My five gray hairs, or ruined fortune, flout,
    With wealth your state, your mind with arts improve,
5       Take you a course, get you a place,
      Observe His Honor, or His Grace,
Or the King's real, or his stampéd face°          *On coins*
    Contémplate; what you will, approve,
    So you will let me love.

10 Alas, alas, who's injured by my love?
    What merchant's ships have my sighs drowned?
Who says my tears have overflowed his ground?
    When did my colds a forward spring remove?
      When did the heats which my veins fill
15       Add one more to the plaguy bill?°     *Weekly list of*
Soldiers find wars, and lawyers find out still    *plague victims*
    Litigious men, which quarrels move,
    Though she and I do love.

Call us what you will, we're made such by love;
20     Call her one, me another fly,
We're tapers too, and at our own cost die,°    *Metaphor for*
    And we in us find th' eagle and the dove.   *sexual intercourse.*
      The phoenix° riddle hath more wit    *A legendary bird*
      By us: we two being one, are it.   *which lived 500 years,*
25 So, to one neutral thing both sexes fit.   *consumed itself in fire,*
    We die and rise the same, and prove   *and rose anew from the*
    Mysterious by this love.                *ashes*

We can die by it, if not live by love,
And if unfit for tombs and hearse
30 Our legend be, it will be fit for verse;
And if no piece of chronicle° we prove, History
We'll build in sonnets pretty rooms;
As well a well-wrought urn becomes
The greatest ashes, as half-acre tombs;
35 And by these hymns, all shall approve
Us canonized for love:

And thus invoke us: You whom reverend love
Made one another's hermitage;
You, to whom love was peace, that now is rage;
40 Who did the whole world's soul contract, and drove
Into the glasses of your eyes
(So made such mirrors, and such spies,
That they did all to you epitomize)
Countries, towns, courts: Beg from above
45 A pattern of your love!


ROBERT GRAVES
*Counting the Beats*

You, love, and I,
(He whispers) you and I,
And if no more than only you and I
What care you or I?

5 Counting the beats,
Counting the slow heart beats,
The bleeding to death of time in slow heart beats,
Wakeful they lie.

Cloudless day,
10 Night, and a cloudless day;
Yet the huge storm will burst upon their heads one day
From a bitter sky.

Where shall we be,
(She whispers) where shall we be,
15 When death strikes home, O where then shall we be
Who were you and I?

14

Not there but here,
(He whispers) only here,
As we are, here, together, now and here,
20  Always you and I.

Counting the beats,
Counting the slow heart beats,
The bleeding to death of time in slow heart beats,
Wakeful they lie.

OLD TESTAMENT*
*From* Song of Songs, *Ch. 4,1–16*

Behold, thou art fair, my love; behold, thou art fair; thou hast doves' eyes within thy locks: thy hair is as a flock of goats, that appear from mount Gilead.

Thy teeth are like a flock of sheep that are even shorn, which came up from the washing; whereof every one bear twins, and none is barren among them.

Thy lips are like a thread of scarlet, and thy speech is comely: thy temples are like a piece of a pomegranate within thy locks.

Thy neck is like the tower of David builded for an armory, whereon there hang a thousand bucklers, all shields of mighty men.

5  Thy two breasts are like two young roes that are twins, which feed among the lilies.

Until the day break, and the shadows flee away, I will get me to the mountains of myrrh, and to the hill of frankincense.

Thou art all fair, my love; there is no spot in thee.

Come with me from Lebanon, my spouse, with me from Lebanon: look from the top of Amana, from the top of Shenir and Hermon, from the lions' dens, from the mountains of the leopards.

Thou hast ravished my heart, my sister, my spouse; thou hast ravished my heart with one of thine eyes, with one chain of thy neck.

10  How fair is thy love, my sister, my spouse! how much better is thy love than wine! and the smell of thine ointments than all spices!

* King James Translation.

Thy lips, O my spouse, drop as the honey-comb: honey and milk are under thy tongue; and the smell of thy garments is like the smell of Lebanon.

A garden inclosed is my sister, my spouse; a spring shut up, a fountain sealed.

Thy plants are an orchard of pomegranates, with pleasant fruits; camphire, with spikenard,

Spikenard and saffron; calamus and cinnamon, with all trees of frankincense; myrrh and aloes, with all the chief spices:

15  A fountain of gardens, a well of living waters, and streams from Lebanon.

Awake, O north wind; and come, thou south; blow upon my garden, that the spices thereof may flow out. Let my beloved come into his garden, and eat his pleasant fruits.


LEROI JONES
*The Clearing*


Trees  & brown squares
of shadow. The green
washed out and drained into clumps of mist
that cloak more trees. And trees, outside
5   the window; or spreading heavy fronds
stepping away from the light. We come
to a forest, or we see it
from the window. We step into it,
spreading the heavy leaves, or drop the blind
10    & let it clatter in the damp breeze from the yard.

Where are the beasts? In a forest,
there are always wild beasts. And the sun, a woman,
goes there to sleep. Brown trunks
their shadows against the white wall, rain
15   spreading against the glass. Blue rain
outside, and shadows against the wall. A wet wind
moves them. The smells
come in. Leaves & darkness
wetting our faces. Breathing
20   through the leaves, and disappear.

Trees,
 & shadows of trees (the wind

pushes them apart. I am
an animal watching
25 his forest. Listening
for your breathing, your merest
move in the dark. You wear
a gown of it. The dark
ness. And
30 we can move naked
through it, through
the forest
if it does not disappear. Who
will remember
35 the way back. When the blind
flings back
and more smells come in. As sound
or light moving against the wall. Where
are the beasts?

40 The eye is useless. Sound, Sound,
& what you smell
or feel. I am someone else
who smells you. The lamp
at the corner is bleak
45 & leafless. Its light
docs not even reach
the edge of the trees.

What bird
makes that noise? (If this
50 were a western place, a temperate hand
could shape it. A western mouth
could make it on this mist. Green mist
settling on our flesh. (if this
were a western place, a bank
55 of the Marne, Cezanne's greens
& yellows floating unreal
under a bridge. A blue bridge
for a temperate eye. We have
vines. (What bird
60 makes that noise?

Your voice down the hall. Are
you singing? A shadow song
we lock our movement

in. Were you singing?
65 down the hall. White plaster
on the walls, our fingers
leave their marks, on
the dust, or tearing
the wall away. Were you
70 singing? What song
was that?

I love you ( & you be
quiet, & feel my wet mouth
on your fingers, I
75 love you
& bring you fish
& oranges. (Before the light fails
we should move to a dryer place,
but not too far from water.) I
80 Love you &
you are singing. What song
is that? (The blinds held up
by a wind, tearing
the shadows. I
85 Love you
& you hide yourself
in the shadows. The forest is huge
around us. The night
clings to our cries. (I hear
90 your voice
down the hall, through the window, above
all those trees, a light
it seems
& you are singing. What song
95 is that The words
are beautiful.

# Section II

## Robert Herrick
### *To Daffodils*

    Fair daffodils, we weep to see
      You haste away so soon:
    As yet the early-rising sun
      Has not attained his noon.
5        Stay, stay,
      Until the hasting day
        Has run
      But to the evensong;
    And, having prayed together, we
10    Will go with you along.
    We have short time to stay as you;
      We have as short a spring;
    As quick a growth to meet decay,
      As you or anything.
15       We die,
      As your hours do, and dry
        Away
    Like to the summer's rain;
    Or as the pearls of morning's dew,
20    Ne'er to be found again.


## William Wordsworth
### *I Wandered Lonely as a Cloud*

    I wandered lonely as a cloud
    That floats on high o'er vales and hills,
    When all at once I saw a crowd,
    A host, of golden daffodils;
5    Beside the lake, beneath the trees,
    Fluttering and dancing in the breeze.

    Continuous as the stars that shine
    And twinkle on the milky way,
    They stretched in never-ending line
10    Along the margin of a bay:
    Ten thousand saw I at a glance,
    Tossing their heads in sprightly dance.

The waves beside them danced; but they
Outdid the sparkling waves in glee;
15  A poet could not but be gay,
In such a jocund company;
I gazed—and gazed—but little thought
What wealth the show to me had brought:

For oft, when on my couch I lie
20  In vacant or in pensive mood,
They flash upon that inward eye
Which is the bliss of solitude;
And then my heart with pleasure fills,
And dances with the daffodils.

## WILLIAM COWPER
*The Poplar Field*

The poplars are felled; farewell to the shade
And the whispering sound of the cool colonnade;
The winds play no longer and sing in the leaves,
Nor Ouse° on his bosom their image receives.         *A river in*
                                                      *northern*
5  Twelve years have elapsed since I first took a view  *England*
Of my favorite field, and the bank where they grew;
And now in the grass behold they are laid,
And the tree is my seat that once lent me a shade.

The blackbird has fled to another retreat,
10  Where the hazels afford him a screen from the heat,
And the scene where his melody charmed me before,
Resounds with his sweet-flowing ditty no more.

My fugitive years are all hasting away,
And I must ere long lie as lowly as they,
15  With a turf on my breast, and a stone at my head,
Ere another such grove shall arise in its stead.

'Tis a sight to engage me, if anything can,
To muse on the perishing pleasures of man;

Though his life be a dream, his enjoyments, I see,
20    Have a being less durable even than he.


GERARD MANLEY HOPKINS
*Binsey Poplars*
Felled 1879

My aspens dear, whose airy cages quelled,
Quelled or quenched in leaves the leaping sun,
All felled, felled, are all felled;
    Of a fresh and following folded rank°          *Row of trees with*
5              Not spared, not one          *alternate trees set off at*
        That dandled a sandalled                        *an angle*
    Shadow that swam or sank
On meadow and river and wind-wandering weed-winding bank.

O if we but knew what we do
10        When we delve or hew—
    Hack and rack the growing green!
        Since country is so tender
    To touch, her being só slender,
    That, like this sleek and seeing ball°          *The eye*
15    But a prick will make no eye at all,
    Where we, even where we mean
            To mend her we end her,
        When we hew or delve:
After-comers cannot guess the beauty been.
20    Ten or twelve, only ten or twelve
        Strokes of havoc únselve
        The sweet especial scene,
    Rural scene, a rural scene,
    Sweet especial rural scene.

GERARD MANLEY HOPKINS
*The Caged Skylark*

As a dare-gale skylark scanted° in a dull cage          *Stinted*
    Man's mounting spirit in his bone-house, mean house,
    dwells—

That bird beyond the remembering his free fells;
This in drudgery, day-laboring-out life's age.

5    Though aloft on turf or perch or poor low stage,
      Both sing sometimes the sweetest, sweetest spells,
      Yet both droop deadly sometimes in their cells
Or wring their barriers in bursts of fear or rage.

Not that the sweet-fowl, song-fowl, needs no rest—
10   Why, hear him, hear him babble and drop down to his nest,
      But his own nest, wild nest, no prison.

Man's spirit will be flesh-bound when found at best,
But uncumbered: meadow-down is not distressed
      For a rainbow footing it nor he for his bones risen.


## PERCY BYSSHE SHELLEY
### *To a Skylark*

Hail to thee, blithe Spirit!
    Bird thou never wert,
That from Heaven, or near it,
    Pourest thy full heart
5  In profuse strains of unpremeditated art.

Higher still and higher
    From the earth thou springest
Like a cloud of fire;
    The blue deep thou wingest,
10  And singing still dost soar, and soaring ever singest.

In the golden lightning
    Of the sunken sun,
O'er which clouds are bright'ning,
    Thou dost float and run;
15  Like an unbodied joy whose race is just begun.

The pale purple even
    Melts around thy flight;
Like a star of Heaven,
    In the broad daylight
20  Thou art unseen, but yet I hear thy shrill delight,

Keen as are the arrows
　　Of that silver sphere,
Whose intense lamp narrows
　　In the white dawn clear
25　Until we hardly see—we feel that it is there.

All the earth and air
　　With thy voice is loud,
As, when night is bare,
　　From one lonely cloud
30　The moon rains out her beams, and Heaven is overflowed.

What thou art we know not;
　　What is most like thee?
From rainbow clouds there flow not
　　Drops so bright to see
35　As from thy presence showers a rain of melody.

Like a Poet hidden
　　In the light of thought,
Singing hymns unbidden,
　　Till the world is wrought
40　To sympathy with hopes and fears it heeded not:

Like a high-born maiden
　　In a palace tower,
Soothing her love-laden
　　Soul in secret hour
45　With music sweet as love, which overflows her bower:

Like a glowworm golden
　　In a dell of dew,
Scattering unbeholden
　　Its aërial hue
50　Among the flowers and grass, which screen it from the view!

Like a rose embowered
　　In its own green leaves,
By warm winds deflowered,
　　Till the scent it gives
55　Makes faint with too much sweet those heavy-wingéd thieves:

Sound of vernal showers
　　On the twinkling grass,

Rain-awakened flowers,
 All that ever was
60 Joyous, and clear, and fresh, thy music doth surpass:

 Teach us, Sprite° or Bird,         *Spirit*
  What sweet thoughts are thine:
 I have never heard
  Praise of love or wine
65 That panted forth a flood of rapture so divine.

 Chorus Hymeneal,°          *Wedding song*
  Or triumphal chant,
 Matched with thine would be all
  But an empty vaunt,
70 A thing wherein we feel there is some hidden want.

 What objects are the fountains
  Of thy happy strain?
 What fields, or waves, or mountains?
  What shapes of sky or plain?
75 What love of thine own kind? what ignorance of pain?

 With thy clear keen joyance
  Languor cannot be:
 Shadow of annoyance
  Never came near thee:
80 Thou lovest—but ne'er knew love's sad satiety.

 Waking or asleep,
  Thou of death must deem
 Things more true and deep
  Than we mortals dream,
85 Or how could thy notes flow in such a crystal stream?

 We look before and after,
  And pine for what is not:
 Our sincerest laughter
  With some pain is fraught;
90 Our sweetest songs are those that tell of saddest thought.

 Yet if we could scorn
  Hate, and pride, and fear;
 If we were things born
  Not to shed a tear,
95 I know not how thy joy we ever should come near.

Better than all measures
  Of delightful sound,
Better than all treasures
  That in books are found,
100 Thy skill to poet were, thou scorner of the ground!

Teach me half the gladness
  That thy brain must know,
Such harmonious madness
  From my lips would flow
105 The world should listen then—as I am listening now.


# THOMAS HARDY
*Shelley's Skylark*
(The neighborhood of Leghorn: March 1887)

Somewhere afield here something lies
In Earth's oblivious eyeless trust
That moved a poet to prophecies—
A pinch of unseen, unguarded dust:

5   The dust of the lark that Shelley heard,
And made immortal through times to be;—
Though it only lived like another bird,
And knew not its immortality:

Lived its meek life; then, one day, fell—
10  A little ball of feather and bone;
And how it perished, when piped farewell,
And where it wastes, are alike unknown.

Maybe it rests in the loam I view,
Maybe it throbs in a myrtle's green,
15  Maybe it sleeps in the coming hue
Of a grape on the slopes of yon inland scene.

Go find it, faeries, go and find
That tiny pinch of priceless dust,
And bring a casket silver-lined,
20  And framed of gold that gems encrust;

And we will lay it safe therein,
And consecrate it to endless time;
For it inspired a bard to win
Ecstatic heights in thought and rhyme.

THOMAS HARDY
*The Darkling Thrush*

I leant upon a coppice° gate      *Thicket or wood consisting of*
    When Frost was spectre-gray,      *small trees*
And Winter's dregs made desolate
    The weakening eye of day.
5 The tangled bine-stems° scored the sky      *Stems of a climbing*
    Like strings of broken lyres,      *plant*
And all mankind that haunted nigh
    Had sought their household fires.

The land's sharp features seemed to be
10     The Century's corpse outleant,
His crypt the cloudy canopy,
    The wind his death-lament.
The ancient pulse of germ and birth
    Was shrunken hard and dry,
15 And every spirit upon earth
    Seemed fervourless as I.

At once a voice arose among
    The bleak twigs overhead
In a full-hearted evensong
20     Of joy illimited;
An aged thrush, frail, gaunt, and small,
    In blast-beruffled plume,
Had chosen thus to fling his soul
    Upon the growing gloom.

25 So little cause for carolings
    Of such ecstatic sound
Was written on terrestrial things
    Afar or nigh around,

That I could think there trembled through
30      His happy good-night air
Some blessed Hope, whereof he knew
      And I was unaware.


ALICE MEYNELL
*A Thrush Before Dawn*

A voice peals in this end of night
    A phrase of notes resembling stars,
Single and spiritual notes of light.
    What call they at my window bars?
5      The South, the past, the day to be,
      An ancient infelicity.

Darkling, deliberate, what sings
    This wonderful one, alone, at peace?
What wilder things than song, what things
10    Sweeter than youth, clearer than Greece,
      Dearer than Italy, untold
      Delight, and freshness centuries old?

And first first-loves, a multitude,
    The exaltation of their pain;
15  Ancestral childhood long renewed;
    And midnights of invisible rain;
      And gardens, gardens, night and day,
      Gardens and childhood all the way.

What Middle Ages passionate,
20    O passionless voice! What distant bells
Lodged in the hills, what palace state
    Illyrian! For it speaks, it tells,
      Without desire, without dismay
      Some morrow and some yesterday.

25  All-natural things! But more—Whence came
    This yet remoter mystery?
How do these starry notes proclaim
    A graver still divinity?
      This hope, this sanctity of fear?
30      *O innocent throat! O human ear!*

# Edward Taylor
## Upon a Spider Catching a Fly

Thou sorrow, venom elf:
   Is this thy play,
To spin a web out of thyself
   To catch a fly?
5     For why?

I saw a pettish wasp
   Fall foul therein,
Whom yet thy whorl-pins° did not clasp       *Here, the spider's*
   Lest he should fling                           *legs*
10   His sting.

But as afraid, remote
   Didst stand hereat
And with thy little fingers stroke
   And gently tap
15   His back.

Thus gently him didst treat
   Lest he should pet,
And in a froppish,° waspish heat                *Fretful*
   Should greatly fret
20   Thy net.

Whereas the silly fly,
   Caught by its leg
Thou by the throat tookst hastily
   And hind the head
25   Bite dead.

This goes to pot,° that not                *Deteriorates*
   Nature doth call.
Strive not above what strength hath got
   Lest in the brawl
30   Thou fall.

This fray seems thus to us.
   Hell's spider gets
His entrails spun to whip-cords thus,
   And wove to nets
35   And sets.

To tangle Adam's race
   In's stratagems
To their destructions, spoiled, made base
   By venom things,
40        Damned sins.

But mighty, gracious Lord
   Communicate
Thy grace to break the cord, afford
   Us glory's gate
45        And state.

We'll nightingale sing like
   When perched on high
In glory's cage, thy glory, bright,
   And thankfully,
50        For joy.


ROBERT LOWELL
*Mr. Edwards and the Spider* *

I saw the spiders marching through the air,
Swimming from tree to tree that mildewed day
   In latter August when the hay
   Came creaking to the barn. But where
5        The wind is westerly,
   Where gnarled November makes the spiders fly
   Into the apparitions of the sky,
   They purpose nothing but their ease and die
Urgently beating east to sunrise and the sea;

10        What are we in the hands of the great God?
   It was in vain you set up thorn and briar
      In battle array against the fire
      And treason crackling in your blood;
      For the wild thorns grow tame
15    And will do nothing to oppose the flame;
   Your lacerations tell the losing game
   You play against a sickness past your cure.
How will the hands be strong? How will the heart endure?

* Jonathan Edwards, Puritan divine, who, at the age of twelve, wrote an essay
on flying spiders.

A very little thing, a little worm,
20   Or hourglass-blazoned spider, it is said,
        Can kill a tiger. Will the dead
        Hold up his mirror and affirm
            To the four winds the smell
        And flash of his authority? It's well
25   If God who holds you to the pit of hell,
        Much as one holds a spider, will destroy,
Baffle and dissipate your soul. As a small boy

        On Windsor Marsh, I saw the spider die
        When thrown into the bowels of fierce fire:
30       There's no long struggle, no desire
        To get up on its feet and fly—
            It stretches out its feet
        And dies. This is the sinner's last retreat;
        Yes, and no strength exerted on the heat
35       Then sinews the abolished will, when sick
And full of burning, it will whistle on a brick.

        But who can plumb the sinking of that soul?
        Josiah Hawley,° picture yourself cast      *An uncle of Edwards*
        Into a brick-kiln where the blast      *who committed suicide*
40       Fans your quick vitals to a coal—
            If measured by a glass,
        How long would it seem burning! Let there pass
        A minute, ten, ten trillion, but the blaze
        Is infinite, eternal; this is death,
45   To die and know it. This is the Black Widow, death.


WALT WHITMAN
*A Noiseless Patient Spider*


        A noiseless patient spider,
        I mark'd where on a little promontory it stood isolated,
        Mark'd how to explore the vacant vast surrounding,
        It launch'd forth filament, filament, filament, out of itself,
5    Ever unreeling them, ever tirelessly speeding them.

        And you O my soul where you stand,
        Surrounded, detached, in measureless oceans of space,
        Ceaselessly musing, venturing, throwing, seeking the spheres to
            connect them,

Till the bridge you will need be form'd, till the
    ductile° anchor hold,                                    *Pliant*
10 Till the gossamer thread you fling catch somewhere, O my soul.

MATTHEW ARNOLD
*Dover Beach*

The sea is calm tonight.
The tide is full, the moon lies fair
Upon the straits; on the French coast the light
Gleams and is gone; the cliffs of England stand,
5 Glimmering and vast, out in the tranquil bay.
Come to the window, sweet is the night-air!
Only, from the long line of spray
Where the sea meets the moon-blanched land,
Listen! you hear the grating roar
10 Of pebbles which the waves draw back, and fling,
At their return, up the high strand,
Begin, and cease, and then again begin,
With tremulous cadence slow, and bring
The eternal note of sadness in.

15 Sophocles long ago
Heard it on the Aegean, and it brought
Into his mind the turbid ebb and flow
Of human misery; we
Find also in the sound a thought,
20 Hearing it by this distant northern sea.

The Sea of Faith
Was once, too, at the full, and round earth's shore
Lay like the folds of a bright girdle furled.
But now I only hear
25 Its melancholy, long, withdrawing roar,
Retreating, to the breath
Of the night-wind, down the vast edges drear
And naked shingles of the world.

Ah, love, let us be true
30 To one another! for the world, which seems

To lie before us like a land of dreams,
So various, so beautiful, so new,
Hath really neither joy, nor love, nor light,
Nor certitude, nor peace, nor help for pain;
35 And we are here as on a darkling plain
Swept with confused alarms of struggle and flight,
Where ignorant armies clash by night.


# GERARD MANLEY HOPKINS
## God's Grandeur

The world is charged with the grandeur of God.
It will flame out, like shining from shook foil;
It gathers to a greatness, like the ooze of oil
Crushed.° Why do men then now not reck° his rod?          *I.e.,*
5 Generations have trod, have trod, have trod;          *crushed from*
And all is seared with trade; bleared, smeared with          *olives.*
     toil;          *Understand, recognize*
And wears man's smudge and shares man's smell: the soil
Is bare now, nor can foot feel, being shod.
And for all this, nature is never spent;
10 There lives the dearest freshness deep down things;
And though the last lights off the black West went
Oh, morning, at the brown brink eastward, springs—
Because the Holy Ghost over the bent
World broods with warm breast and with ah! bright wings.

# THOMAS GRAY
## Ode on a Distant Prospect of Eton College

Ἄνθρωπος· ἱκανὴ πρόφασις εἰς τὸ δυστυχεῖν.*
—MENANDER

Ye distant spires, ye antique towers,
   That crown the watery glade,
Where grateful Science° still adores          *Learning*
   Her Henry's holy shade,†

* I am a man, and that is reason enough for being miserable.
† Henry VI, founder of Eton.

*34*

5   And ye, that from the stately brow
      Of Windsor's heights the expanse below
         Of grove, of lawn, of mead survey,
      Whose turf, whose shade, whose flowers among
      Wanders the hoary Thames along
10       His silver-winding way.

      Ah happy hills, ah pleasing shade,
         Ah fields beloved in vain,
      Where once my careless childhood strayed,
         A stranger yet to pain!
15   I feel the gales, that from ye blow,
      A momentary bliss bestow,
         As waving fresh their gladsome wing,
      My weary soul they seem to soothe,
      And, redolent of joy and youth,
20       To breathe a second spring.

      Say, Father Thames, for thou hast seen
         Full many a sprightly race
      Disporting on thy margent green
         The paths of pleasure trace,
25   Who foremost now delight to cleave
      With pliant arm thy glassy wave?
         The captive linnet which enthrall?°                    *Imprison*
      What idle progeny succeed*
      To chase the rolling circle's° speed,                     *The hoop*
30       Or urge the flying ball?

      While some on earnest business bent
         Their murmuring labors ply
      'Gainst graver hours, that bring constraint
         To sweeten liberty:
35   Some bold adventurers disdain
      The limits of their little reign,
         And unknown regions dare descry:°                      *Discover*
      Still as they run they look behind,
      They hear a voice in every wind,
40       And snatch a fearful joy.

      Gay hope is theirs by fancy fed,
         Less pleasing when possessed;

* Follow the example of the preceding generation.

The tear forgot as soon as shed,
  The sunshine of the breast:
45 Theirs buxom° health of rosy hue,                    *Vigorous*
Wild wit, invention ever new,
  And lively cheer of vigor born;
The thoughtless day, the easy night,
The spirits pure, the slumbers light,
50   That fly the approach of morn.

Alas, regardless of their doom,
  The little victims play!
No sense have they of ills to come,
  Nor care beyond today.
55 Yet see how all around 'em wait
The ministers of human fate,
  And black Misfortune's baleful train!
Ah, show them where in ambush stand
To seize their prey the murderous band!
60   Ah, tell them they are men!

These shall the fury Passions tear,
  The vultures of the mind,
Disdainful Anger, pallid Fear,
  And Shame that skulks behind;
65 Or pining Love shall waste their youth,
Or Jealousy with rankling tooth,
  That inly gnaws the secret heart,
And Envy wan, and faded Care,
Grim-visaged comfortless Despair,
70   And Sorrow's piercing dart.

Ambition this° shall tempt to rise,              *I.e., one of them*
  Then whirl the wretch from high,
To bitter Scorn a sacrifice,
  And grinning Infamy.
75 The stings of Falsehood those° shall try,            *I.e., others*
And hard Unkindness' altered eye,
  That mocks the tear it forced to flow;
And keen Remorse with blood defiled,
And moody Madness laughing wild
80   Amid severest woe.

Lo, in the vale of years beneath
  A grisly troop are seen,

The painful family of Death,
　　More hideous than their queen:
85 This racks the joints, this fires the veins,
That every laboring sinew strains,
　　Those in the deeper vitals rage:
Lo, Poverty, to fill the band,
That numbs the soul with icy hand,
90 　　And slow-consuming Age.


To each his sufferings: all are men,
　　Condemned alike to groan;
The tender for another's pain,
　　The unfeeling for his own.
95 Yet ah! why should they know their fate?
Since sorrow never comes too late,
　　And happiness too swiftly flies.
Thought would destroy their paradise.
No more; where ignorance is bliss,
100 　　'Tis folly to be wise.


WILLIAM WORDSWORTH

*Lines*

Composed a Few Miles Above Tintern Abbey on
Revisiting the Banks of the Wye During a Tour.
July 13, 1798


　　Five years have passed; five summers, with the length
Of five long winters! and again I hear
These waters, rolling from their mountain-springs
With a soft inland murmur. Once again
5 Do I behold these steep and lofty cliffs,
That on a wild secluded scene impress
Thoughts of more deep seclusion; and connect
The landscape with the quiet of the sky.
The day is come when I again repose
10 Here, under this dark sycamore, and view
These plots of cottage ground, these orchard tufts,
Which at this season, with their unripe fruits,
Are clad in one green hue, and lose themselves
'Mid groves and copses. Once again I see
15 These hedgerows, hardly hedgerows, little lines

Of sportive wood run wild; these pastoral farms,
Green to the very door; and wreaths of smoke
Sent up, in silence, from among the trees!
With some uncertain notice, as might seem
20   Of vagrant dwellers in the houseless woods,
Or of some Hermit's cave, where by his fire
The Hermit sits alone.
                              These beauteous forms,
Through a long absence, have not been to me
As is a landscape to a blind man's eye;
25   But oft, in lonely rooms, and 'mid the din
Of towns and cities, I have owed to them,
In hours of weariness, sensations sweet,
Felt in the blood, and felt along the heart;
And passing even into my purer mind,
30   With tranquil restoration—feelings too
Of unremembered pleasure; such, perhaps,
As have no slight or trivial influence
On that best portion of a good man's life,
His little, nameless, unremembered, acts
35   Of kindness and of love. Nor less, I trust,
To them I may have owed another gift,
Of aspect more sublime; that blessed mood,
In which the burthen of the mystery,
In which the heavy and the weary weight
40   Of all this unintelligible world,
Is lightened—that serene and blessed mood,
In which the affections gently lead us on—
Until, the breath of this corporeal frame
And even the motion of our human blood
45   Almost suspended, we are laid asleep
In body, and become a living soul;
While with an eye made quiet by the power
Of harmony, and the deep power of joy,
We see into the life of things.
                                        If this
50   Be but a vain belief, yet, oh! how oft—
In darkness and amid the many shapes
Of joyless daylight; when the fretful stir
Unprofitable, and the fever of the world,
Have hung upon the beatings of my heart—
55   How oft, in spirit, have I turned to thee,
O sylvan Wye! thou wanderer through the woods,
How often has my spirit turned to thee!

And now, with gleams of half-extinguished thought,
With many recognitions dim and faint,
60 And somewhat of a sad perplexity,
The picture of the mind revives again;
While here I stand, not only with the sense
Of present pleasure, but with pleasing thoughts
That in this moment there is life and food
65 For future years. And so I dare to hope,
Though changed, no doubt, from what I was when first
I came among these hills; when like a roe
I bounded o'er the mountains, by the sides
Of the deep rivers, and the lonely streams,
70 Wherever nature led—more like a man
Flying from something that he dreads than one
Who sought the thing he loved. For nature then
(The coarse° pleasures of my boyish days,          *I.e., primarily*
And their glad animal movements all gone by)          *physical*
75 To me was all in all.—I cannot paint
What then I was. The sounding cataract
Haunted me like a passion; the tall rock,
The mountain, and the deep and gloomy wood,
Their colors and their forms, were then to me
80 An appetite; a feeling and a love,
That had no need of a remoter charm,
By thought supplied, nor any interest
Unborrowed from the eye.—That time is past,
And all its aching joys are now no more,
85 And all its dizzy raptures. Not for this
Faint° I, nor mourn nor murmur; other gifts          *Become*
Have followed; for such loss, I would believe,          *discouraged*
Abundant recompense. For I have learned
To look on nature, not as in the hour
90 Of thoughtless youth; but hearing oftentimes
The still, sad music of humanity,
Nor harsh nor grating, though of ample power
To chasten and subdue. And I have felt
A presence that disturbs me with the joy
95 Of elevated thoughts; a sense sublime
Of something far more deeply interfused,
Whose dwelling is the light of setting suns,
And the round ocean and the living air,
And the blue sky, and in the mind of man:
100 A motion and a spirit, that impels
All thinking things, all objects of all thought,

And rolls through all things. Therefore am I still
A lover of the meadows and the woods,
And mountains; and of all that we behold
105 From this green earth; of all the mighty world
Of eye, and ear—both what they half create,
And what perceive; well pleased to recognize
In nature and the language of the sense
The anchor of my purest thoughts, the nurse,
110 The guide, the guardian of my heart, and soul
Of all my moral being.

                 Nor perchance,
If I were not thus taught, should I the more
Suffer my genial spirits° to decay:           *Vital energies*
For thou art with me here upon the banks
115 Of this fair river; thou my dearest Friend,°    *Wordsworth's*
My dear, dear Friend; and in thy voice I catch   *sister, Dorothy*
The language of my former heart, and read
My former pleasures in the shooting lights
Of thy wild eyes. Oh! yet a little while
120 May I behold in thee what I was once,
My dear, dear Sister! and this prayer I make,
Knowing that Nature never did betray
The heart that loved her; 'tis her privilege,
Through all the years of this our life, to lead
125 From joy to joy: for she can so inform
The mind that is within us, so impress
With quietness and beauty, and so feed
With lofty thoughts, that neither evil tongues,
Rash judgments, nor the sneers of selfish men,
130 Nor greetings where no kindness is, nor all
The dreary intercourse of daily life,
Shall e'er prevail against us, or disturb
Our cheerful faith, that all which we behold
Is full of blessings. Therefore let the moon
135 Shine on thee in thy solitary walk;
And let the misty mountain winds be free
To blow against thee: and, in after years,
When these wild ecstasies shall be matured
into a sober pleasure; when thy mind
140 Shall be a mansion for all lovely forms,
Thy memory be as a dwelling place
For all sweet sounds and harmonies; oh! then,
If solitude, or fear, or pain, or grief
Should be thy portion, with what healing thoughts

145 Of tender joy wilt thou remember me,
   And these my exhortations! Nor, perchance—
   If I should be where I no more can hear
   Thy voice, nor catch from thy wild eyes these gleams
   Of past existence—wilt thou then forget
150 That on the banks of this delightful stream
   We stood together; and that I, so long
   A worshiper of Nature, hither came
   Unwearied in that service; rather say
   With warmer love—oh! with far deeper zeal
155 Of holier love. Nor wilt thou then forget,
   That after many wanderings, many years
   Of absence, these steep woods and lofty cliffs,
   And this green pastoral landscape, were to me
   More dear, both for themselves and for thy sake!

ANDREW MARVELL
*The Mower Against Gardens*

   Luxurious man, to bring his vice in use,
      Did after him the world seduce,
   And from the fields the flowers and plants allure,
      When nature was most plain and pure.
5  He first enclosed within the garden's square
      A dead and standing pool of air;
   And a more luscious earth for them did knead,
      Which stupefied them while it fed.
   The pink° grew then as double as his mind;     *A kind of flower*
10    The nutriment did change the kind.
   With strange perfumes he did the roses taint;
      And flowers themselves were taught to paint.
   The tulip, white, did for complexion seek,
      And learned to interline its cheek;
15 Its onion root they then so high did hold
      That one was for a meadow sold.
   Another world was searched, through oceans new,
      To find the marvel of Peru.°               *A kind of flower*
   And yet these rarities might be allowed
20    To man, that sov'reign thing and proud,

Had he not dealt between the bark and tree,
　　Forbidden mixtures there to see.
No plant now knew the stock from which it came;
　　He grafts upon the wild the tame,
25　That the uncertain and adult'rate fruit
　　Might put the palate in dispute.
His green seraglio° has its eunuchs too,　　　*A place where a sultan*
　　Lest any tyrant him outdo;　　　　　　　*keeps his wives; harem;*
And in the cherry he does nature vex,　　　　*here, the garden*
30　To procreate without a sex.
'Tis all enforced, the fountain and the grot,
　　While the sweet fields do lie forgot,
Where willing nature does to all dispense
　　A wild and fragrant innocence;
35　And fauns and fairies do the meadows till
　　More by their presence than their skill.
Their statues, polished by some ancient hand,
　　May to adorn the gardens stand;
But howsoe'er the figures do excel,
40　The gods themselves with us do dwell.


# E. E. CUMMINGS
*pity this busy monster, manunkind*

pity this busy monster, manunkind,

not. Progress is a comfortable disease:
your victim (death and life safely beyond)

plays with the bigness of his littleness
5　—electrons deify one razorblade
into a mountainrange; lenses extend

unwish through curving wherewhen till unwish
returns on its unself.
　　　　　　　　A world of made
is not a world of born—pity poor flesh

10　and trees, poor stars and stones, but never this
fine specimen of hypermagical

ultraomnipotence. We doctors know

a hopeless case if—listen: there's a hell
of a good universe next door; let's go

# Section III

## WILLIAM WORDSWORTH
### The World Is Too Much with Us

The world is too much with us; late and soon,
Getting and spending, we lay waste our powers;
Little we see in Nature that is ours;
We have given our hearts away, a sordid boon!
5 This Sea that bares her bosom to the moon,
The winds that will be howling at all hours,
And are up-gathered now like sleeping flowers,
For this, for everything, we are out of tune;
It moves us not.—Great God! I'd rather be
10 A Pagan suckled in a creed outworn;
So might I, standing on this pleasant lea,
Have glimpses that would make me less forlorn;
Have sight of Proteus rising from the sea;
Or hear old Triton° blow his wreathéd horn.   *Sea gods from*
*Greek mythology*

## EDGAR ALLAN POE
### Sonnet—To Science

Science! true daughter of Old Time thou art!
    Who alterest all things with thy peering eyes.
Why preyest thou thus upon the poet's heart,
    Vulture, whose wings are dull realities?
5 How should he love thee? or how deem thee wise?
    Who wouldst not leave him in his wandering
To seek for treasure in the jeweled skies,
    Albeit he soared with an undaunted wing?
Hast thou not dragged Diana°            *Roman goddess of the hunt;*
    from her car?                       *her car is the moon.*
10    And driven the Hamadryad° from the wood   *Wood nymph*
To seek a shelter in some happier star?   *who lives in a tree.*
    Hast thou not torn the Naiad° from her flood,   *River nymph*
The Elfin from the green grass, and from me
The summer dream beneath the tamarind tree?°   *Oriental tree*

## ROBINSON JEFFERS
### Science

Man, introverted man, having crossed
In passage and but a little with the nature of things this latter
    century

Has begot giants; but being taken up
Like a maniac with self-love and inward conflicts cannot
    manage his hybrids.
5   Being used to deal with edgeless dreams,
Now he's bred knives on nature turns them also inward: they
    have thirsty points though.
His mind forebodes his own destruction;
Actæon who saw the goddess naked among leaves and his
    hounds tore him.
A little knowledge, a pebble from the shingle,
10  A drop from the oceans: who would have dreamed this
    infinitely little too much?

## WALT WHITMAN
### *To a Locomotive in Winter*

Thee for my recitative,
Thee in the driving storm even as now, the snow, the winter-day
    declining,
Thee in thy panoply,° thy measur'd dual throbbing    *Armor*
    and thy beat convulsive,
Thy black cylindric body, golden brass and silvery steel,
5   Thy ponderous side-bars, parallel and connecting rods, gyrating,
    shuttling at thy sides,
Thy metrical, now swelling pant and roar, now tapering in the
    distance,
Thy great protruding head-light fix'd in front,
Thy long, pale, floating vapor-pennants, tinged with delicate
    purple,
The dense and murky clouds out-belching from thy smoke-stack,
10  Thy knitted frame, thy springs and valves, the tremulous twinkle
    of thy wheels,
Thy train of cars behind, obedient, merrily following,
Through gale or calm, now swift, now slack, yet steadily careering;
Type of the modern—emblem of motion and power—pulse of
    the continent,
For once come serve the Muse and merge in verse, even as here
    I see thee,
15  With storm and buffeting gusts of wind and falling snow,
By day thy warning ringing bell to sound its notes,
By night thy silent signal lamps to swing.

Fierce-throated beauty!
Roll through my chant with all thy lawless music, thy swinging
 lamps at night,
20 Thy madly-whistled laughter, echoing, rumbling like an earth-
 quake, rousing all,
Law of thyself complete, thine own track firmly holding,
(No sweetness debonair of tearful harp or glib piano thine,)
Thy trills of shrieks by rocks and hills return'd,
Launch'd o'er the prairies wide, across the lakes,
25 To the free skies unpent and glad and strong.


EMILY DICKINSON
*I Like to See It Lap the Miles*

### 585

I like to see it lap the Miles—
And lick the Valleys up—
And stop to feed itself at Tanks—
And then—prodigious step

5 Around a Pile of Mountains—
And supercilious peer
In Shanties—by the sides of Roads—
And then a Quarry pare

To fit its sides
10 And crawl between
Complaining all the while
In horrid—hooting stanza—
Then chase itself down Hill—

And neigh like Boanerges°    *A loud vociferous preacher*
15 Then—prompter than a Star
Stop—docile and omnipotent
At its own stable door—


STEPHEN SPENDER
*The Express*

After the first powerful plain manifesto
The black statement of pistons, without more fuss

47

But gliding like a queen, she leaves the station.
Without bowing and with restrained unconcern
5    She passes the houses which humbly crowd outside,
The gasworks and at last the heavy page
Of death, printed by gravestones in the cemetery.
Beyond the town there lies the open country
Where, gathering speed, she acquires mystery,
10   The luminous self-possession of ships on ocean.
It is now she begins to sing—at first quite low
Then loud, and at last with a jazzy madness—
The song of her whistle screaming at curves,
Of deafening tunnels, brakes, innumerable bolts.
15   And always light, aerial, underneath
Goes the elate meter of her wheels.
Steaming through metal landscape on her lines
She plunges new eras of wild happiness
Where speed throws up strange shapes, broad curves
20   And parallels clean like the steel of guns.
At last, further than Edinburgh or Rome,
Beyond the crest of the world, she reaches night
Where only a low streamline brightness
Of phosphorus on the tossing hills is white.
25   Ah, like a comet through flames she moves entranced
Wrapt in her music no bird song, no, nor bough
Breaking with honey buds, shall ever equal.


CARL SANDBURG
*Limited*

I am riding on a limited express, one of the crack trains of the
       nation.
Hurtling across the prairie into blue haze and dark air go fifteen
       all-steel coaches holding a thousand people.
(All the coaches shall be scrap and rust and all the men and
       women laughing in the diners and sleepers shall pass to
       ashes.)
I ask a man in the smoker where he is going and he answers:
       "Omaha."

# T. S. ELIOT
## *Preludes*

### 1

The winter evening settles down
With smell of steaks in passageways.
Six o'clock.
The burnt-out ends of smoky days.
5  And now a gusty shower wraps
The grimy scraps
Of withered leaves about your feet
And newspapers from vacant lots;
The showers beat
10  On broken blinds and chimney-pots,
And at the corner of the street
A lonely cab-horse steams and stamps.
And then the lighting of the lamps.

### 2

The morning comes to consciousness
15  Of faint stale smells of beer
From the sawdust-trampled street
With all its muddy feet that press
To early coffee-stands.
With the other masquerades
20  That time resumes,
One thinks of all the hands
That are raising dingy shades
In a thousand furnished rooms.

### 3

You tossed a blanket from the bed,
25  You lay upon your back, and waited;
You dozed, and watched the night revealing
The thousand sordid images
Of which your soul was constituted;
They flickered against the ceiling.
30  And when all the world came back
And the light crept up between the shutters
And you heard the sparrows in the gutters,
You had such a vision of the street
As the street hardly understands;
35  Sitting along the bed's edge, where
You curled the papers from your hair,

Or clasped the yellow soles of feet
In the palms of both soiled hands.

4

His soul stretched tight across the skies
40   That fade behind a city block,
Or trampled by insistent feet
At four and five and six o'clock;
And short square fingers stuffing pipes,
And evening newspapers, and eyes
45   Assured of certain certainties,
The conscience of a blackened street
Impatient to assume the world.

I am moved by fancies that are curled
Around these images, and cling:
50   The notion of some infinitely gentle
Infinitely suffering thing.

Wipe your hand across your mouth, and laugh;
The worlds revolve like ancient women
Gathering fuel in vacant lots.


HART CRANE
*Proem: To Brooklyn Bridge*
*From* The Bridge

How many dawns, chill from his rippling rest
The seagull's wings shall dip and pivot him,
Shedding white rings of tumult, building high
Over the chained bay waters Liberty—

5   Then, with inviolate curve, forsake our eyes
As apparitional as sails that cross
Some page of figures to be filed away;
—Till elevators drop us from our day . . .

I think of cinemas, panoramic sleights
10   With multitudes bent toward some flashing scene
Never disclosed, but hastened to again,
Foretold to other eyes on the same screen;

And Thee, across the harbor, silver-paced
As though the sun took step of thee, yet left
15  Some motion ever unspent in thy stride—
Implicitly thy freedom staying thee!

Out of some subway scuttle, cell or loft
A bedlamite speeds to thy parapets,
Tilting there momently, shrill shirt ballooning,
20  A jest falls from the speechless caravan.

Down Wall, from girder into street noon leaks,
A rip-tooth of the sky's acetylene,
All afternoon the cloud-flown derricks turn . . .
Thy cables breathe the North Atlantic still.

25  And obscure as that heaven of the Jews,
Thy guerdon . . . Accolade thou dost bestow
Of anonymity time cannot raise:
Vibrant reprieve and pardon thou dost show.

O harp and altar, of the fury fused,
30  (How could mere toil align thy choiring strings!)
Terrific threshold of the prophet's pledge,
Prayer of pariah, and the lover's cry—

Again the traffic lights that skim thy swift
Unfractioned idiom, immaculate sigh of stars,
35  Beading thy path—condense eternity:
And we have seen night lifted in thine arms.

Under thy shadow by the piers I waited;
Only in darkness is thy shadow clear.
The City's fiery parcels all undone,
40  Already snow submerges an iron year . . .

O Sleepless as the river under thee,
Vaulting the sea, the prairies' dreaming sod,
Unto us lowliest sometime sweep, descend
And of the curveship lend a myth to God.

## Vladimir Mayakovsky
*Brooklyn Bridge*
*Translated by Max Hayward and George Reavey*

    Give, Coolidge,
    a shout of joy!
    I too will spare no words
              about good things.
5  Blush
       at my praise,
            go red as our flag,
    however
         united-states
10                 -of
  -america you may be.
  As a crazed believer
          enters
             a church,
15  retreats
       into a monastery cell,
               austere and plain;
  so I,
     in graying evening
20             haze,
  humbly set foot
         on Brooklyn Bridge.
  As a conqueror presses
           into a city
25              all shattered,
  on cannon with muzzles
          craning high as a giraffe—
  so, drunk with glory
         eager to live,
30  I clamber,
       in pride,
         upon Brooklyn Bridge.
  As a foolish painter
        plunges his eye,
35  sharp and loving,
         into a museum madonna,
  so I,
    from the near skies
         bestrewn with stars,

40 gaze
        at New York
                        through the Brooklyn Bridge.
    New York,
                heavy and stifling
45                              till night,
    has forgotten
                its hardships
                            and height;
    and only
50          the household ghosts
    ascend
            in the lucid glow of its windows.
    Here
        the elevateds
55                      drone softly.
    And only
                their gentle
                            droning
    tell us:
60          here trains
                        are crawling and rattling
    like dishes
                being cleared into a cupboard.
    While
65          a shopkeeper fetched sugar
    from a mill
                that seemed to project
                                    out of the water—
    the masts
70          passing under the bridge
    looked
            no larger than pins.
    I am proud
                of just this
75                              mile of steel;
    upon it,
            my visions come to life, erect—
    here's a fight
                for construction
80                                  instead of style,
    an austere disposition
                        of bolts
                            and steel.

If
85    the end of the world
                              befall—
and chaos
               smash our planet
                              to bits,
90   and what remains
                         ˙will be
                                   this
bridge, rearing above the dust of destruction;
then,
95        as huge ancient lizards
                              are rebuilt
from bones
             finer than needles,
                              to tower in museums,
100  so,
        from this bridge,
                           a geologist of the centuries
will succeed
             in recreating
105                              our contemporary world.
He will say:
                —Yonder paw
                              of steel
once joined
             the seas and the prairies;
110  from this spot,
                   Europe
                           rushed to the West,
scattering
             to the wind
115                        Indian feathers.
This rib
          reminds us
                      of a machine—
120  just imagine,
                   would there be hands enough,
after planting
               a steel foot
                           in Manhattan,
125  to yank
          Brooklyn to oneself
                              by the lip?

By the cables
                    of electric strands,
130 I recognize
                    the era succeeding
                                        the steam age—
here
        men
135             had ranted
                            on radio.
Here
        men
                had ascended
140                         in planes.
For some,
            life
                    here
                        had no worries;
145 for others,
                it was a prolonged
                                and hungry howl.
From this spot,
                    jobless men
150 leapt
            headlong
                    into the Hudson.
Now
        my canvas
155                 is unobstructed
as it stretches on cables of string
                                    to the feet of the stars.
I see:
        here
160             stood Mayakovsky,
stood,
            composing verse, syllable by syllable.
I stare
        as an Eskimo gapes at a train,
165 I seize on it
                as a tick fastens to an ear.
Brooklyn Bridge—
yes . . .
            That's quite a thing!

# Walt Whitman
## *Crossing Brooklyn Ferry*

Flood-tide below me! I see you face to face!
Clouds of the west—sun there half an hour high—I see you also
    face to face.

Crowds of men and women attired in the usual costumes, how
    curious you are to me!
On the ferry-boats the hundreds and hundreds that cross, returning
    home, are more curious to me than you suppose,
5  And you that shall cross from shore to shore years hence are more
    to me, and more in my meditations, than you might suppose.

## 2

The impalpable sustenance of me from all things at all hours of
    the day,
The simple, compact, well-join'd scheme, myself disintegrated,
    every one disintegrated yet part of the scheme,
The similitudes of the past and those of the future,
The glories strung like beads on my smallest sights and hearings,
    on the walk in the street and the passage over the river,
10  The current rushing so swiftly and swimming with me far away,
The others that are to follow me, the ties between me and them,
The certainty of others, the life, love, sight, hearing of others.

Others will enter the gates of the ferry and cross from shore to
    shore,
Others will watch the run of the flood-tide,
15  Others will see the shipping of Manhattan north and west, and
    the heights of Brooklyn to the south and east,
Others will see the islands large and small;
Fifty years hence, others will see them as they cross, the sun half
    an hour high,
A hundred years hence, or ever so many hundred years hence,
    others will see them,
Will enjoy the sunset, the pouring-in of the flood-tide, the
    falling-back to the sea of the ebb-tide.

## 3

20  It avails not, time nor place—distance avails not,
I am with you, you men and women of a generation, or ever so
    many generations hence,

Just as you feel when you look on the river and sky, so I felt,
Just as any of you is one of a living crowd, I was one of a crowd,
Just as you are refresh'd by the gladness of the river and the bright
flow, I was refresh'd,
25 Just as you stand and lean on the rail, yet hurry with the swift
current, I stood yet was hurried,
Just as you look on the numberless masts of ships and the thick-
stemm'd pipes of steamboats, I look'd.


I too many and many a time cross'd the river of old,
Watched the Twelfth-month sea-gulls, saw them high in the air
floating with motionless wings, oscillating their bodies,
Saw how the glistening yellow lit up parts of their bodies and
left the rest in strong shadow,
30 Saw the slow-wheeling circles and the gradual edging toward
the south,
Saw the reflection of the summer sky in the water,
Had my eyes dazzled by the shimmering track of beams,
Look'd at the fine centrifugal spokes of light round the shape of
my head in the sunlit water,
Look'd on the haze on the hills southward and south-westward,
35 Look'd on the vapor as it flew in fleeces tinged with violet,
Look'd toward the lower bay to notice the vessels arriving,
Saw their approach, saw aboard those that were near me,
Saw the white sails of schooners and sloops, saw the ships at
anchor,
The sailors at work in the rigging or out astride the spars,
40 The round masts, the swinging motion of the hulls, the slender
serpentine pennants,
The large and small steamers in motion, the pilots in their pilot-
houses,
The white wake left by the passage, the quick tremulous whirl of
the wheels,
The flags of all nations, the falling of them at sunset,
The scallop-edged waves in the twilight, the ladled cups, the
frolicsome crests and glistening,
45 The stretch afar growing dimmer and dimmer, the gray walls of
the granite storehouses by the docks,
On the river the shadowy group, the big steam-tug closely
flank'd on each side by the barges, the hay-boat, the belated
lighter,
On the neighboring shore the fires from the foundry chimneys
burning high and glaringly into the night,

Casting their flicker of black contrasted with wild red and yellow
    light over the tops of houses, and down into the clefts of
    streets.

### 4

These and all else were to me the same as they are to you,
50  I loved well those cities, loved well the stately and rapid river,
The men and women I saw were all near to me,
Others the same—others who look back on me because I look'd
    forward to them,
(The time will come, though I stop here to-day and to-night.)

### 5

What is it then between us?
55  What is the count of the scores or hundreds of years between
    us?

Whatever it is, it avails not—distance avails not, and place avails
    not,
I too lived, Brooklyn of ample hills was mine,
I too walk'd the streets of Manhattan island, and bathed in the
    waters around it,
I too felt the curious abrupt questionings stir within me,
60  In the day among crowds of people sometimes they came upon
    me,
In my walks home late at night or as I lay in my bed they came
    upon me,
I too had been struck from the float forever held in solution,
I too had receiv'd identity by my body,
That I was I knew was of my body, and what I should be I knew
    I should be of my body.

### 6

65  It is not upon you alone the dark patches fall,
The dark threw its patches down upon me also,
The best I had done seem'd to me blank and suspicious,
My great thoughts as I supposed them, were they not in reality
    meagre?
Nor is it you alone who know what it is to be evil,
70  I am he who knew what it was to be evil,
I too knitted the old knot of contrariety,
Blabb'd, blush'd, resented, lied, stole, grudg'd,
Had guile, anger, lust, hot wishes I dared not speak,
Was wayward, vain, greedy, shallow, sly, cowardly, malignant,

75 The wolf, the snake, the hog, not wanting in me,
The cheating look, the frivolous word, the adulterous wish, not
wanting,
Refusals, hates, postponements, meanness, laziness, none of these
wanting,
Was one with the rest, the days and haps of the rest,
Was call'd by my nighest name by clear loud voices of young
men as they saw me approaching or passing,
80 Felt their arms on my neck as I stood, or the negligent leaning of
their flesh against me as I sat,
Saw many I loved in the street or ferry-boat or public assembly,
yet never told them a word,
Lived the same life with the rest, the same old laughing, gnawing,
sleeping,
Play'd the part that still looks back on the actor or actress,
The same old role, the role that is what we make it, as great as
we like,
85 Or as small as we like, or both great and small.


7

Closer yet I approach you,
What thought you have of me now, I had as much of you—I
laid in my stores in advance,
I consider'd long and seriously of you before you were born.

Who was to know what should come home to me?
90 Who knows but I am enjoying this?
Who knows, for all the distance, but I am as good as looking at
you now, for all you cannot see me?


8

Ah, what can ever be more stately and admirable to me than
mast-hemm'd Manhattan?
River and sunset and scallop-edg'd waves of flood-tide?
The sea-gulls oscillating their bodies, the hay-boat in the twilight,
and the belated lighter?
95 What gods can exceed these that clasp me by the hand, and with
voices I love call me promptly and loudly by my nighest
name as I approach?
What is more subtle than this which ties me to the woman or
man that looks in my face?
Which fuses me into you now, and pours my meaning into
you?

We understand then do we not?
What I promis'd without mentioning it, have you not accepted?
100  What the study could not teach—what the preaching could not
  accomplish is accomplish'd, is it not?

### 9

Flow on, river! flow with the flood-tide, and ebb with the ebb-
  tide!
Frolic on, crested and scallop-edg'd waves!
Gorgeous clouds of the sunset! drench with your splendor me,
  or the men and women generations after me!
Cross from shore to shore, countless crowds of passengers!
105  Stand up, tall masts of Mannahatta! stand up, beautiful hills of
  Brooklyn!
Throb, baffled and curious brain! throw out questions and
  answers!
Suspend here and everywhere, eternal float of solution!
Gaze, loving and thirsting eyes, in the house or street or public
  assembly!
Sound out, voices of young men! loudly and musically call me
  by my nighest name!
110  Live, old life! play the part that looks back on the actor or actress!
Play the old role, the role that is great or small according as one
  makes it!
Consider, you who peruse me, whether I may not in unknown
  ways be looking upon you;
Be firm, rail over the river, to support those who lean idly, yet
  haste with the hasting current;
Fly on, sea-birds! fly sideways, or wheel in large circles high in
  the air;
115  Receive the summer sky, you water, and faithfully hold it till all
  downcast eyes have time to take it from you!
Diverge, fine spokes of light, from the shape of my head, or any
  one's head, in the sunlit water!
Come on, ships from the lower bay! pass up or down, white-
  sail'd, schooners, sloops, lighters!
Flaunt away, flags of all nations! be duly lower'd at sunset!
Burn high your fires, foundry chimneys! cast black shadows at
  nightfall! cast red and yellow light over the tops of the
  houses!
120  Appearances, now or henceforth, indicate what you are,
You necessary film, continue to envelop the soul,
About my body for me, and your body for you, be hung our
  divinest aromas,

Thrive, cities—bring your freight, bring your shows, ample and
　　sufficient rivers,
Expand, being than which none else is perhaps more spiritual,
125 Keep your places, objects than which none else is more lasting.

You have waited, you always wait, you dumb, beautiful ministers,
We receive you with free sense at last, and are insatiate hencefor-
　　ward,

Not you any more shall be able to foil us, or withhold yourselves
　　from us,
We use you, and do not cast you aside—we plant you permanently
　　within us,
130 We fathom you not—we love you—there is perfection in you
　　also,
You furnish your parts toward eternity,
Great or small, you furnish your parts toward the soul.

Anonymous
*Scottsboro*
*American Negro; collected 1936*

Paper come out—done strewed de news
Seven po' chillun moan deat' house blues,
Seven po' chillun moanin' deat' house blues.
Seven nappy heads wit' big shiny eye
5 All boun' in jail and framed to die,
All boun' in jail and framed to die.

Messin' white woman—snake lyin' tale
Hang and burn and jail wit' no bail.
Dat hang and burn and jail wit' no bail.
10 Worse ol' crime in white folks' lan'
Black skin coverin' po' workin' man,
Black skin coverin' po' workin' man.

Judge and jury—all in de stan'
Lawd, biggety name for same lynchin' ban',
15 Lawd, biggety name for same lynchin' ban'.

White folks and nigger in great co't house
Like cat down cellar wit' nohole mouse.
Like cat down cellar wit' nohole mouse.


COUNTEE CULLEN
*Scottsboro, Too, Is Worth Its Song*
(A Poem to American Poets)


I said:
Now will the poets sing,—
Their cries go thundering
Like blood and tears
5  Into the nation's ears,
Like lightning dart
Into the nation's heart.
Against disease and death and all things fell,
And war,
10  Their strophes° rise and swell          *Stanzas*
To jar
The foe smug in his citadel.


Remembering their sharp and pretty
Tunes for Sacco and Vanzetti,°    *Italian anarchists executed in*
15  I said:                    *1920 after a controversial murder*
Here too's a cause divinely spun              *trial*
For those whose eyes are on the sun,
Here in epitome
Is all disgrace
20  And epic wrong,
Like wine to brace
The minstrel heart, and blare it into song.


Surely, I said,
Now will the poets sing.
25    But they have raised no cry.
    I wonder why.

# PERCY BYSSHE SHELLEY
## Song to the Men of England

Men of England, wherefore plough
For the lords who lay ye low?
Wherefore weave with toil and care
The rich robes your tyrants wear?

5 Wherefore feed, and clothe, and save,
From the cradle to the grave,
Those ungrateful drones who would
Drain your sweat—nay, drink your blood?

Wherefore, Bees of England, forge
10 Many a weapon, chain, and scourge,
That these stingless drones may spoil
The forced produce of your toil?

Have ye leisure, comfort, calm,
Shelter, food, love's gentle balm?
15 Or what is it ye buy so dear
With your pain and with your fear?

The seed ye sow, another reaps;
The wealth ye find, another keeps;
The robes ye weave, another wears;
20 The arms ye forge, another bears.

Sow seed,—but let no tyrant reap;
Find wealth,—let no impostor heap;
Weave robes,—let not the idle wear;
Forge arms,—in your defence to bear.

25 Shrink to your cellars, holes, and cells;
In halls ye deck, another dwells.
Why shake the chains ye wrought? Ye see
The steel ye tempered glance on ye.

With plough and spade, and hoe and loom,
30 Trace your grave, and build your tomb,
And weave your winding-sheet, till fair
England be your sepulchre.

## Robert Burns
### *Scots, Wha Hae*

Scots, wha hae wi' Wallace bled,
Scots, wham Bruce has aften led,
Welcome to your gory bed,
  Or to victorie.

5  Now's the day, and now's the hour;
See the front o' battle lour;
See approach proud Edward's power—
  Chains and slaverie!

Wha will be a traitor-knave?
10  Wha can fill a coward's grave?
Wha sae base as be a slave?
  Let him turn and flee!

Wha for Scotland's King and law
Freedom's sword will strongly draw,
15  Freeman stand, or freeman fa',
  Let him follow me!

By oppression's woes and pains!
By your sons in servile chains!
We will drain our dearest veins,
20   But they shall be free!

Lay the proud usurpers low!
Tyrants fall in every foe!
Liberty's in every blow!
  Let us do, or die!


## Claude McKay
### *If We Must Die*

If we must die, let it not be like hogs
Hunted and penned in an inglorious spot,
While round us bark the mad and hungry dogs,
Making their mock at our accursèd lot.
5  If we must die, O let us nobly die,
So that our precious blood may not be shed

In vain; then even the monsters we defy
Shall be constrained to honor us though dead!
O kinsmen we must meet the common foe!
10 Though far outnumbered let us show us brave,
And for their thousand blows deal one deathblow!
What though before us lies the open grave?
Like men we'll face the murderous, cowardly pack,
Pressed to the wall, dying, but fighting back!

CARL SANDBURG
*The People Will Live On*
*From* The People, Yes

        The people will live on.
The learning and blundering people will live on.
        They will be tricked and sold and again sold
And go back to the nourishing earth for rootholds,
5        The people so peculiar in renewal and comback,
        You can't laugh off their capacity to take it.
The mammoth rests between his cyclonic dramas.

The people so often sleepy, weary, enigmatic,
is a vast huddle with many units saying:
10        "I earn my living.
        I make enough to get by
        and it takes all my time.
        If I had more time
        I could do more for myself
15        and maybe for others.
        I could read and study
        and talk things over
        and find out about things.
        It takes time.
20        I wish I had the time."

The people is a tragic and comic two-face:
hero and hoodlum: phantom and gorilla twist-
ing to moan with a gargoyle mouth: "They
buy me and sell me . . . it's a game . . .
25 sometime I'll break loose . . ."

Once having marched
Over the margins of animal necessity,
Over the grim line of sheer subsistence
Then man came
30    To the deeper rituals of his bones,
To the lights lighter than any bones,
To the time for thinking things over,
To the dance, the song, the story,
Or the hours given over to dreaming,
35          Once having so marched.


Between the finite limitations of the five senses
and the endless yearnings of man for the beyond
the people hold to the humdrum bidding of work and food
while reaching out when it comes their way
40    for lights beyond the prison of the five senses,
for keepsakes lasting beyond any hunger or death.
This reaching is alive.
The panderers and liars have violated and smutted it.
Yet this reaching is alive yet
45          for lights and keepsakes.


The people know the salt of the sea
and the strength of the winds
lashing the corners of the earth.
The people take the earth
50    as a tomb of rest and a cradle of hope.
Who else speaks for the Family of Man?
They are in tune and step
with constellations of universal law.


The people is a polychrome,°                    *Varicolored*
55  a spectrum and a prism
held in a moving monolith,
a console organ of changing themes,
a clavilux° of color poems                      *A kind of organ which*
wherein the sea offers fog                      *simultaneously produces*
60  and the fog moves off in rain               *music and projects colors*
and the labrador sunset shortens                        *on a screen*
to a nocturne of clear stars
serene over the shot spray
of northern lights.

65  The steel mill sky is alive.
    The fire breaks white and zigzag
    shot on a gun-metal gloaming.
    Man is a long time coming.
    Man will yet win.
70  Brother may yet line up with brother:

    This old anvil laughs at many broken hammers.
        There are men who can't be bought.
        The fireborn are at home in fire.
        The stars make no noise.
75      You can't hinder the wind from blowing.
        Time is a great teacher.
        Who can live without hope?
    In the darkness with a great bundle of grief the people march.
    In the night, and overhead a shovel of stars for keeps, the people
        march:
80              "Where to? what next?"


EDWIN MARKHAM
*The Man with the Hoe*
(Written after seeing Millet's world-famous painting)

    Bowed by the weight of centuries he leans
    Upon his hoe and gazes on the ground,
    The emptiness of ages in his face,
    And on his back the burden of the world.
5   Who made him dead to rapture and despair,
    A thing that grieves not and that never hopes,
    Stolid and stunned, a brother to the ox?
    Who loosened and let down this brutal jaw?
    Whose was the hand that slanted back this brow?
10  Whose breath blew out the light within this brain?

    Is this the Thing the Lord God made and gave
    To have dominion over sea and land;
    To trace the stars and search the heavens for power;
    To feel the passion of Eternity?
15  Is this the dream He dreamed who shaped the suns
    And marked their ways upon the ancient deep?
    Down all the caverns of Hell to their last gulf
    There is no shape more terrible than this—

More tongued with censure of the world's blind greed—
20  More filled with signs and portents for the soul—
More packt with danger to the universe.

What gulfs between him and the seraphim!
Slave of the wheel of labor, what to him
Are Plato and the swing of Pleiades?
25  What the long reaches of the peaks of song,
The rift of dawn, the reddening of the rose?
Through this dread shape the suffering ages look;
Time's tragedy is in that aching stoop;
Through this dread shape humanity betrayed,
30  Plundered, profaned, and disinherited,
Cries protest to the Judges of the World,
A protest that is also prophecy.

O masters, lords and rulers in all lands,
Is this the handiwork you give to God,
35  This monstrous thing distorted and soul-quenched?
How will you ever straighten up this shape;
Touch it again with immortality;
Give back the upward looking and the light;
Rebuild in it the music and the dream;
40  Make right the immemorial infamies,
Perfidious wrongs, immedicable woes?

O masters, lords and rulers in all lands,
How will the Future reckon with this man?
How answer his brute question in that hour
45  When whirlwinds of rebellion shake all shores?
How will it be with kingdoms and with kings—
With those who shaped him to the thing he is—
When this dumb terror shall rise to judge the world,
After the silence of the centuries?

WILLIAM BLAKE
*London*

I wander thro' each charter'd° street,                    *Legally defined*
Near where the charter'd Thames does flow,

And mark in every face I meet
Marks of weakness, marks of woe.

5   In every cry of every man,
In every Infant's cry of fear,
In every voice, in every ban,°          *A law or notice commanding*
The mind-forg'd manacles I hear.                    *or forbidding*

How the Chimney-sweeper's cry
10  Every blackning Church appalls;
And the hapless Soldier's sigh
Runs in blood down Palace walls.

But most thro' midnight streets I hear
How the youthful Harlot's curse
15  Blasts the new-born Infant's tear,
And blights with plagues the Marriage hearse.


BYRON BLACK
*I, the Fake Mad Bomber and Walking It Home Again*

First comes the cold,
and puffing as classes change
fast as the frames of a film
and dried old sarcophagi° of professors reel on          *Stone coffins*
5   trot placidly Latin with its dust and their rot.

Then dives the red sun
crashes like the stock market, in black
"the day was fine" as Wm. says
and the Tower stands impudent, one wants to slap it down
10  before the blast-off into stone-gray space.

Brisk bright day
Wm. and I walking fast,
we smile at lurid tales which shock like adders

Dark people with the faces of bulldogs
15  gruffly waddle past, Chryslers with the scream of a rocket
charge us jousting, we hurry fast
to the flap and claw of the Night Hawk

where dark hamburgers from the heart of a living vulture
are served by an Aztec princess
20 "the hamburger don't come with onions"
(pimples as jewels, and the pop of gum)
And the white bourgeois, slimy smiles
slide in with assuredness of talkative slugs, to music of the bank

outside the brightwork of their gaudy Cadillacs
25 wails like a chrome banshee toward the cool evening, and sad
     glass eyes,
And I thanking Wm. we part
he for home
and I full of cheer and good meat

head for my place, legs flashing
30 the power of wet muscles
sends an electric orgasm,
and as approaching Red River, now dry
beside the stadium where Christians are devourers
the night breaks
35 I know myself as the Fake Mad Bomber
and light a black cigar in the dark to prove it.

# T. S. Eliot
## The Love Song of J. Alfred Prufrock

*S'io credesse che mia risposta fosse*
*A persona che mai tornasse al mondo,*
*Questa fiamma staria senza piu scosse.*
*Ma perciocche giammai di questo fondo*
*Non torno vivo alcun, s'i'odo il vero,*
*Senza tema d'infamia ti rispondo.** *

Let us go then, you and I,
When the evening is spread out against the sky
Like a patient etherized upon a table;

* Dante, *Inferno*, XXVII, 61–66. "If I thought my answer were to one who ever could return to the world, this flame should shake no more; but since none ever did return alive from this depth, if what I hear be true, without fear of infamy I answer thee."

Let us go, through certain half-deserted streets,
5 The muttering retreats
Of restless nights in one-night cheap hotels
And sawdust restaurants with oyster-shells:
Streets that follow like a tedious argument
Of insidious intent
10 To lead you to an overwhelming question. . .
Oh, do not ask, "What is it?"
Let us go and make our visit.

In the room the women come and go
Talking of Michelangelo.

15 The yellow fog that rubs its back upon the window-panes
The yellow smoke that rubs its muzzle on the window-panes
Licked its tongue into the corners of the evening,
Lingered upon the pools that stand in drains,
Let fall upon its back the soot that falls from chimneys,
20 Slipped by the terrace, made a sudden leap,
And seeing that it was a soft October night,
Curled once about the house, and fell asleep.

And indeed there will be time
For the yellow smoke that slides along the street,
25 Rubbing its back upon the window-panes;
There will be time, there will be time
To prepare a face to meet the faces that you meet;
There will be time to murder and create,
And time for all the works and days of hands
30 That lift and drop a question on your plate;
Time for you and time for me,
And time yet for a hundred indecisions,
And for a hundred visions and revisions,
Before the taking of a toast and tea.

35 In the room the women come and go
Talking of Michelangelo.

And indeed there will be time
To wonder, "Do I dare?" and, "Do I dare?"
Time to turn back and descend the stair,
40 With a bald spot in the middle of my hair—
[They will say: "How his hair is growing thin!"]

My morning coat, my collar mounting firmly to the chin,
My necktie rich and modest, but asserted by a simple pin—
[They will say: "But how his arms and legs are thin!"]
45 Do I dare
Disturb the universe?
In a minute there is time
For decisions and revisions which a minute will reverse.

For I have known them all already, known them all:
50 Have known the evenings, mornings, afternoons,
I have measured out my life with coffee spoons;
I know the voices dying with a dying fall
Beneath the music from a farther room.
    So how should I presume?

55 And I have known the eyes already, known them all—
The eyes that fix you in a formulated phrase,
And when I am formulated, sprawling on a pin,
When I am pinned and wriggling on the wall,
Then how should I begin
60 To spit out all the butt-ends of my days and ways?
    And how should I presume?

And I have known the arms already, known them all—
Arms that are braceleted and white and bare
[But in the lamplight, downed with light brown hair!]
65 Is it perfume from a dress
That makes me so digress?
Arms that lie along a table, or wrap about a shawl.
    And should I then presume?
    And how should I begin?

                    . . . . .

70 Shall I say, I have gone at dusk through narrow streets
And watched the smoke that rises from the pipes
Of lonely men in shirt-sleeves, leaning out of windows? . . .

I should have been a pair of ragged claws
Scuttling across the floors of silent seas.

                    . . . . .

75 And the afternoon, the evening, sleeps so peacefully!
Smoothed by long fingers,
Asleep . . . tired . . . or it malingers,
Stretched on the floor, here beside you and me.

Should I, after tea and cakes and ices,
80  Have the strength to force the moment to its crisis?
But though I have wept and fasted, wept and prayed,
Though I have seen my head [grown slightly bald] brought in
        upon a platter,
I am no prophet—and here's no great matter;
I have seen the moment of my greatness flicker,
85  And I have seen the eternal Footman hold my coat, and snicker,
And in short, I was afraid.

And would it have been worth it, after all,
After the cups, the marmalade, the tea,
Among the porcelain, among some talk of you and me,
90  Would it have been worth while,
To have bitten off the matter with a smile,
To have squeezed the universe into a ball
To roll it toward some overwhelming question,
To say: "I am Lazarus, come from the dead,
95  Come back to tell you all, I shall tell you all"—
If one, settling a pillow by her head,
        Should say: "That is not what I meant at all.
        That is not it, at all."

And would it have been worth it, after all,
100  Would it have been worth while,
After the sunsets and the dooryards and the sprinkled streets,
After the novels, after the teacups, after the skirts that trail along
        the floor—
And this, and so much more?—
It is impossible to say just what I mean!
105  But as if a magic lantern threw the nerves in patterns on a
        screen:
Would it have been worth while
If one, settling a pillow or throwing off a shawl,
And turning toward the window, should say:
        "That is not it at all,
110  That is not what I meant, at all."

                    . . . . .

No! I am not Prince Hamlet, nor was meant to be;
Am an attendant lord, one that will do
To swell a progress,° start a scene or two,          *In Elizabethan*
Advise the prince; no doubt, an easy tool,       *sense: state journey*
115  Deferential, glad to be of use,
Politic, cautious, and meticulous;

Full of high sentence,° but a bit obtuse;          *Sententiousness*
At times, indeed, almost ridiculous—
Almost, at times, the Fool.

120  I grow old . . . I grow old . . .
I shall wear the bottoms of my trousers rolled.

Shall I part my hair behind? Do I dare to eat a peach?
I shall wear white flannel trousers, and walk upon the beach.
I have heard the mermaids singing, each to each.

125  I do not think that they will sing to me.

I have seen them riding seaward on the waves
Combing the white hair of the waves blown back
When the wind blows the water white and black.

We have lingered in the chambers of the sea
130  By sea-girls wreathed with seaweed red and brown
Till human voices wake us, and we drown.


EDWIN ARLINGTON ROBINSON
*Mr. Flood's Party*

Old Eben Flood, climbing alone one night
Over the hill between the town below
And the forsaken upland hermitage
That held as much as he should ever know
5  On earth again of home, paused warily.
The road was his with not a native near;
And Eben, having leisure, said aloud,
For no man else in Tilbury Town to hear:

"Well, Mr. Flood, we have the harvest moon
10  Again, and we may not have many more;
The bird is on the wing, the poet says,
And you and I have said it here before.
Drink to the bird." He raised up to the light
The jug that he had gone so far to fill,
15  And answered huskily: "Well, Mr. Flood,
Since you propose it, I believe I will."

Alone, as if enduring to the end
A valiant armor of scarred hopes outworn,
He stood there in the middle of the road
20 Like Roland's ghost winding a silent horn.
Below him, in the town among the trees,
Where friends of other days had honored him,
A phantom salutation of the dead
Rang thinly till old Eben's eyes were dim.

25 Then, as a mother lays her sleeping child
Down tenderly, fearing it may awake,
He set the jug down slowly at his feet
With trembling care, knowing that most things break;
And only when assured that on firm earth
30 It stood, as the uncertain lives of men
Assuredly did not, he paced away,
And with his hand extended paused again:

"Well, Mr. Flood, we have not met like this
In a long time; and many a change has come
35 To both of us, I fear, since last it was
We had a drop together. Welcome home!"
Convivially returning with himself,
Again he raised the jug up to the light;
And with an acquiescent quaver said:
40 "Well, Mr. Flood, if you insist, I might.

"Only a very little, Mr. Flood—
For auld lang syne. No more, sir; that will do."
So, for the time, apparently it did,
And Eben evidently thought so too;
45 For soon amid the silver loneliness
Of night he lifted up his voice and sang,
Secure, with only two moons listening,
Until the whole harmonious landscape rang—

"For auld lang syne." The weary throat gave out,
50 The last word wavered; and the song being done,
He raised again the jug regretfully
And shook his head, and was again alone.
There was not much that was ahead of him,
And there was nothing in the town below—
55 Where strangers would have shut the many doors
That many friends had opened long ago.

## WILLIAM STAFFORD
### Returned to Say

When I face north a lost Cree
on some new shore puts a moccasin down,
rock in the light and noon for seeing,
he in a hurry and I beside him.

5   It will be a long trip; he will be a new chief;
we have drunk new water from an unnamed stream;
under little dark trees he is to find a path
we both must travel because we have met.

Henceforth we gesture even by waiting;
10  there is a grain of sand on his knifeblade
so small he blows it and while his breathing
darkens the steel his eyes become set

And start a new vision: the rest of his life.
We will mean what he does. Back of this page
15  the path turns north. We are looking for a sign.
Our moccasins do not mark the ground.


## DEAN DETER
### A Letter to One of the Pre-historic Indians Who Built the Mounds at Circleville, Ohio
for Fred Eckman

*1*

safe in your pre-history
without stealth
you paddled down the Scioto
folding lean brown legs
5  into your white canoe.

lean, brown, you folded
into your squaw's white inner leg
nights
you weren't hunting.

10  same passion.

*76*

long into my history
I creep, browneyed,
into those same cottonwoods.


you listened, once,
15  for a bird, high
in that willow.

pointing my white arm
upstream
I tramp on your burial mound
20  whistling (hands cupped on a leaf),
looking for a stone,
a date,
something to bring
me to you,
25  you to me,
the river more blue
like the movies,
the town less real
than it is.

# Section IV

# CHARLES CAUSLEY
## *Recruiting Drive*

Under the willow the willow
    I heard the butcher-bird sing,
Come out you fine young fellow
    From under your mother's wing.
5  I'll show you the magic garden
    That hangs in the beamy air,
The way of the lynx and the angry Sphinx
    And the fun of the freezing fair.

Lie down lie down with my daughter
10    Beneath the Arabian tree,
Gaze on your face in the water
    Forget the scribbling sea.
Your pillow the nine bright shiners
    Your bed the spilling sand,
15  But the terrible toy of my lily-white boy
    Is the gun in his innocent hand.

You must take off your clothes for the doctor
    And stand as straight as a pin,
His hand of stone on your white breast-bone
20    Where the bullets all go in.
They'll dress you in lawn and linen
    And fill you with Plymouth gin,
O the devil may wear a rose in his hair
    I'll wear my fine doe-skin.

25  My mother weeps as I leave her
    But I tell her it won't be long,
The murderers wail in Wandsworth Gaol
    But I shoot a more popular song.
Down in the enemy country
30    Under the enemy tree
There lies a lad whose heart has gone bad
    Waiting for me, for me.

He says I have no culture
    And that when I've stormed the pass
35  I shall fall on the farm with a smoking arm
    And ravish his bonny lass.

Under the willow the willow
 Death spreads her dripping wings
And caught in the snare of the bleeding air
40  The butcher-bird sings, sings, sings.


WILFRED OWEN
*Arms and the Boy*

 Let the boy try along this bayonet-blade
 How cold steel is, and keen with hunger of blood;
 Blue with all malice, like a madman's flash;
 And thinly drawn with famishing for flesh.

5 Lend him to stroke these blind, blunt bullet-heads
 Which long to nuzzle in the heart of lads,
 Or give him cartridges of fine zinc teeth,
 Sharp with the sharpness of grief and death.

 For his teeth seem for laughing round an apple.
10 There lurk no claws behind his fingers supple;
 And god will grow no talons at his heels,
 Nor antlers through the thickness of his curls.

RANDALL JARRELL
*The Death of the Ball Turret Gunner*

 From my mother's sleep I fell into the State,
 And I hunched in its belly till my wet fur froze.
 Six miles from earth, loosed from its dream of life,
 I woke to black flak and the nightmare fighters.
5 When I died they washed me out of the turret with a hose.


WILLIAM BUTLER YEATS
*An Irish Airman Foresees His Death*

 I know that I shall meet my fate
 Somewhere among the clouds above;

Those that I fight I do not hate,
Those that I guard I do not love;
5   My country is Kiltartan Cross,
My countrymen Kiltartan's poor,
No likely end could bring them loss
Or leave them happier than before.
Nor law, nor duty bade me fight,
10   Nor public men, nor cheering crowds,
A lonely impulse of delight
Drove to this tumult in the clouds;
I balanced all, brought all to mind,
The years to come seemed waste of breath,
15   A waste of breath the years behind
In balance with this life, this death.

ALLEN TATE
*Ode to the Confederate Dead*

Row after row with strict impunity
The headstones yield their names to the element,
The wind whirrs without recollection;
In the riven troughs the splayed leaves
5   Pile up, of nature the casual sacrament
To the seasonal eternity of death;
Then driven by the fierce scrutiny
Of heaven to their election in the vast breath,
They sough the rumor of mortality.

10   Autumn is desolation in the plot
Of a thousand acres where these memories grow
From the inexhaustible bodies that are not
Dead, but feed the grass row after rich row.
Think of the autumns that have come and gone!
15   Ambitious November with the humors of the year,
With a particular zeal for every slab,
Staining the uncomfortable angels that rot
On the slabs, a wing chipped here, an arm there:
The brute curiosity of an angel's stare
20   Turns you, like them, to stone,

Transforms the heaving air
Till plunged to a heavier world below
You shift your sea-space blindly
Heaving, turning like the blind crab.

25     Dazed by the wind, only the wind
       The leaves flying, plunge

You know who have waited by the wall
The twilight certainty of an animal,
Those midnight restitutions of the blood
30 You know—the immitigable° pines, the smoky frieze     *Unvarying*
Of the sky, the sudden call: you know the rage,
The cold pool left by the mounting flood,
Of muted Zeno and Parmenides.°     *Greek philosophers who held*
You who have waited for the angry resolution     *that what is*
35 Of those desires that should be yours tomorrow,     *changeable is*
You know the unimportant shrift of death     *a phantom*
And praise the vision
And praise the arrogant circumstance
Of those who fall
40 Rank upon rank, hurried beyond decision—
Here by the sagging gate, stopped by the wall.

       Seeing, seeing only the leaves
       Flying, plunge and expire

Turn your eyes to the immoderate past,
45 Turn to the inscrutable infantry rising
Demons out of the earth—they will not last.
Stonewall, Stonewall, and the sunken fields of hemp,
Shiloh, Antietam, Malvern Hill, Bull Run.
Lost in that orient of the thick and fast
50 You will curse the setting sun.

       Cursing only the leaves crying
       Like an old man in a storm

You hear the shout, the crazy hemlocks point
With troubled fingers to the silence which
55 Smothers you, a mummy, in time.
                    The hound bitch

Toothless and dying, in a musty cellar
Hears the wind only.

               Now that the salt of their blood
60   Stiffens the saltier oblivion of the sea,
Seals the malignant purity of the flood,
What shall we who count our days and bow
Our heads with a commemorial woe
In the ribboned coats of grim felicity,
65   What shall we say of the bones, unclean,
Whose verdurous anonymity will grow?

The ragged arms, the ragged heads and eyes
Lost in these acres of the insane green?
The gray lean spiders come, they come and go;
70   In a tangle of willows without light
The singular screech-owl's tight
Invisible lyric seeds the mind
With the furious murmur of their chivalry.

           We shall say only the leaves
75        Flying, plunge and expire

We shall say only the leaves whispering
In the improbable mist of nightfall
That flies on multiple wing:
Night is the beginning and the end
80   And in between the ends of distraction
Waits mute speculation, the patient curse
That stones the eyes, or like the jaguar leaps
For his own image in a jungle pool, his victim.

What shall we say who have knowledge
85   Carried to the heart? Shall we take the act
To the grave? Shall we, more hopeful, set up the grave
In the house? The ravenous grave?

          Leave now
The shut gate and the decomposing wall:
90   The gentle serpent, green in the mulberry bush,
Riots with his tongue through the hush—
Sentinel of the grave who counts us all!

# WALT WHITMAN
## *When Lilacs Last in the Dooryard Bloom'd*

### 1

When lilacs last in the dooryard bloom'd,
And the great star early droop'd in the western sky in the night,
I mourn'd, and yet shall mourn with ever-returning spring.

Ever-returning spring, trinity sure to me you bring,
5　Lilac blooming perennial and drooping star in the west,
And thought of him I love.

### 2

O powerful western fallen star!
O shades of night—O moody, tearful night!
O great star disappear'd—O the black murk that hides the star!
10　O cruel hands that hold me powerless—O helpless soul of me!
O harsh surrounding cloud that will not free my soul.

### 3

In the dooryard fronting an old farm-house near the white-wash'd
　　palings,
Stands the lilac-bush tall-growing with heart-shaped leaves of rich
　　green,
With many a pointed blossom rising delicate, with the perfume
　　strong I love,
15　With every leaf a miracle—and from this bush in the dooryard,
With delicate-color'd blossoms and heart-shaped leaves of rich
　　green,
A sprig with its flower I break.

### 4

In the swamp in secluded recesses,
A shy and hidden bird is warbling a song.

20　Solitary the thrush,
The hermit withdrawn to himself, avoiding the settlements,
Sings by himself a song.

Song of the bleeding throat,
Death's outlet song of life, (for well dear brother I know,
25　If thou wast not granted to sing thou would'st surely die.)

## 5

Over the breast of the spring, the land, amid cities,
Amid lanes and through old woods, where lately the violets
    peep'd from the ground, spotting the gray debris,
Amid the grass in the fields each side of the lanes, passing the
    endless grass,
Passing the yellow-spear'd wheat, every grain from its shroud in
    the dark-brown fields uprisen,
30 Passing the apple-tree blows of white and pink in the orchards,
Carrying a corpse to where it shall rest in the grave,
Night and day journeys a coffin.

6

Coffin that passes through lanes and streets,°    *Funeral cortège*
Through day and night with the great cloud    *of Lincoln*
    darkening the land,
35 With the pomp of the inloop'd flags with the cities draped in
    black,
With the show of the States themselves as of crape-veil'd women
    standing,
With processions long and winding and the flambeaus of the night,
With the countless torches lit, with the silent sea of faces and the
    unbared heads,
With the waiting depot, the arriving coffin, and the sombre faces,
40 With dirges through the night, with the thousand voices rising
    strong and solemn,
With all the mournful voices of the dirges pour'd around the coffin,
The dim-lit churches and the shuddering organs—where amid
    these you journey,
With the tolling tolling bells' perpetual clang,
Here, coffin that slowly passes,
45 I give you my sprig of lilac.

7

(Nor for you, for one alone,
Blossoms and branches green to coffins all I bring,
For fresh as the morning, thus would I chant a song for you O
    sane and sacred death.

All over bouquets of roses,
50 O death, I cover you over with roses and early lilies,
But mostly and now the lilac that blooms the first,
Copious I break, I break the sprigs from the bushes,
With loaded arms I come, pouring for you,
For you and the coffins all of you O death.)

## 8

55  O western orb sailing the heaven,
    Now I know what you must have meant as a month since I
       walk'd,
    As I walk'd in silence the transparent shadowy night,
    As I saw you had something to tell as you bent to me night after
       night,
    As you droop'd from the sky low down as if to my side, (while
       the other stars all look'd on,)
60  As we wander'd together the solemn night, (for something I know
       not what kept me from sleep,)
    As the night advanced, and I saw on the rim of the west how full
       you were of woe,
    As I stood on the rising ground in the breeze in the cool transparent
       night,
    As I watch'd where you pass'd and was lost in the netherward
       black of the night,
    As my soul in its trouble dissatisfied sank, as where you sad orb,
65  Concluded, dropt in the night, and was gone.

### 9

    Sing on there in the swamp,
    O singer bashful and tender, I hear your notes, I hear your call,
    I hear, I come presently, I understand you,
    But a moment I linger, for the lustrous star has detain'd me,
70  The star my departing comrade holds and detains me.

### 10

    O how shall I warble myself for the dead one there I loved?
    And how shall I deck my song for the large sweet soul that has
       gone?
    And what shall my perfume be for the grave of him I love?
    Sea-winds blown from east and west,
75  Blown from the Eastern sea and blown from the Western sea, till
       there on the prairies meeting,
    These and with these and the breath of my chant,
    I'll perfume the grave of him I love.

### 11

    O what shall I hang on the chamber walls?
    And what shall the pictures be that I hang on the walls,
80  To adorn the burial-house of him I love?

Pictures of growing spring and farms and homes,
With the Fourth-month eve at sundown, and the gray smoke
  lucid and bright,
With floods of the yellow gold of the gorgeous, indolent, sinking
  sun, burning, expanding the air,
With the fresh sweet herbage under foot, and the pale green
  leaves of the trees prolific,
85 In the distance the flowing glaze, the breast of the river, with a
  wind-dapple here and there,
With ranging hills on the banks, with many a line against the
  sky, and shadows,
And the city at hand with dwellings so dense, and stacks of
  chimneys,
And all the scenes of life and the workshops, and the workmen
  homeward returning.

### 12

Lo, body and soul—this land,
90 My own Manhattan with spires, and the sparkling and hurrying
  tides, and the ships,
The varied and ample land, the South and the North in the light,
  Ohio's shores and flashing Missouri,
And ever the far-spreading prairies cover'd with grass and corn.

Lo, the most excellent sun so calm and haughty,
The violet and purple morn with just-felt breezes,
95 The gentle soft-born measureless light,
The miracle spreading bathing all, the fulfill'd noon,
The coming eve delicious, the welcome night and the stars,
Over my cities shining all, enveloping man and land.

### 13

Sing on, sing on you gray-brown bird,
100 Sing from the swamps, the recesses, pour your chant from the
  bushes,
Limitless out of the dusk, out of the cedars and pines.

Sing on dearest brother, warble your reedy song,
Loud human song, with voice of uttermost woe.

O liquid and free and tender!
105 O wild and loose to my soul—O wondrous singer!
You only I hear—yet the star holds me, (but will soon depart,)
Yet the lilac with mastering odor holds me.

Now while I sat in the day and look'd forth,
In the close of the day with its light and the fields of spring, and
    the farmers preparing their crops,
110  In the large unconscious scenery of my land with its lakes and
    forests,
In the heavenly aerial beauty, (after the perturb'd winds and the
    storms,)
Under the arching heavens of the afternoon swift passing, and
    the voices of children and women.
The many-moving sea-tides, and I saw the ships how they sail'd,
And the summer approaching with richness, and the fields all
    busy with labor,
115  And the infinite separate houses, how they all went on, each with
    its meals and minutia of daily usages,
And the streets how their throbbings throbb'd, and the cities
    pent—lo, then and there,
Falling upon them all and among them all, enveloping me with
    the rest,
Appear'd the cloud, appear'd the long black trail,
And I knew death, its thought, and the sacred knowledge of
    death.

120  Then with the knowledge of death as walking one side of me,
And the thought of death close-walking the other side of me,
And I in the middle as with companions, and as holding the hands
    of companions,
I fled forth to the hiding receiving night that talks not,
Down to the shores of the water, the path by the swamp in the
    dimness,
125  To the solemn shadowy cedars and ghostly pines so still.

And the singer so shy to the rest receiv'd me,
The gray-brown bird I know receiv'd us comrades three,
And he sang the carol of death, and a verse for him I love.

From deep secluded recesses,
130  From the fragrant cedars and the ghostly pines so still,
Came the carol of the bird.

And the charm of the carol rapt me,
As I held as if by their hands my comrades in the night,
And the voice of my spirit tallied the song of the bird.

135    *Come lovely and soothing death,*
*Undulate round the world, serenely arriving, arriving,*
*In the day, in the night, to all, to each,*
*Sooner or later delicate death.*

*Prais'd be the fathomless universe,*
140   *For life and joy, and for objects and knowledge curious,*
*And for love, sweet love—but praise! praise! praise!*
*For the sure-enwinding arms of cool-enfolding death.*

*Dark mother always gliding near with soft feet,*
*Have none chanted for thee a chant of fullest welcome?*
145   *Then I chant it for thee, I glorify thee above all,*
*I bring thee a song that when thou must indeed come, come unfalteringly.*

*Approach strong deliveress,*
*When it is so, when thou hast taken them I joyously sing the dead,*
*Lost in the loving floating ocean of thee,*
150   *Laved in the flood of thy bliss O death.*

*From me to thee glad serenades,*
*Dances for thee I propose saluting thee, adornments and feastings for*
    *thee,*
*And the sights of the open landscape and the high-spread sky are fitting,*
*And life and the fields, and the huge and thoughtful night.*

155   *The night in silence under many a star,*
*The ocean shore and the husky whispering wave whose voice I know,*
*And the soul turning to thee O vast and well-veil'd death,*
*And the body gratefully nestling close to thee.*

*Over the tree-tops I float thee a song,*
160   *Over the rising and sinking waves, over the myriad fields and the*
    *prairies wide,*
*Over the dense-pack'd cities all and the teeming wharves and ways,*
*I float this carol with joy, with joy to thee O death.*

*15*

To the tally of my soul,
Loud and strong kept up the gray-brown bird,
165   With pure deliberate notes spreading filling the night.

Loud in the pines and cedars dim,
Clear in the freshness moist and the swamp-perfume,
And I with my comrades there in the night.

While my sight that was bound in my eyes unclosed,
170  As to long panoramas of visions.


And I saw askant the armies,
I saw as in noiseless dreams hundreds of battle-flags,
Borne through the smoke of the battles and pierc'd with missiles
      I saw them,
And carried hither and yon through the smoke, and torn and
      bloody,
175  And at last but a few shreds left on the staffs, (and all in silence,)
And the staffs all splinter'd and broken.


I saw battle-corpses, myriads of them,
And the white skeletons of young men, I saw them,
I saw the debris and debris of all the slain soldiers of the war,
180  But I saw they were not as was thought,
They themselves were fully at rest, they suffer'd not,
The living remain'd and suffer'd, the mother suffer'd,
And the wife and the child and the musing comrade suffer'd,
And the armies that remain'd suffer'd.


### 16

185  Passing the visions, passing the night,
Passing, unloosing the hold of my comrades' hands,
Passing the song of the hermit bird and the tallying song of my
      soul,
Victorious song, death's outlet song, yet varying ever-altering
      song,
As low and wailing, yet clear the notes, rising and falling, flooding
      the night,
190  Sadly sinking and fainting, as warning and warning, and yet again
      bursting with joy,
Covering the earth and filling the spread of the heaven,
As that powerful psalm in the night I heard from recesses,
Passing, I leave thee lilac with heart-shaped leaves,
I leave thee there in the door-yard, blooming, returning with
      spring.


195  I cease from my song for thee,
From my gaze on thee in the west, fronting the west, communing
      with thee,
O comrade lustrous with silver face in the night.

Yet each to keep and all, retrievements out of the night,
The song, the wondrous chant of the gray-brown bird,
200 And the tallying chant, the echo arous'd in my soul,
With the lustrous and drooping star with the countenance full of
   woe,
With the holders holding my hand nearing the call of the bird,
Comrades mine and I in the midst, and their memory ever to
   keep, for the dead I loved so well,
For the sweetest, wisest soul of all my days and lands—and this
   for his dear sake,
205 Lilac and star and bird twined with the chant of my soul,
There in the fragrant pines and the cedars dusk and dim.

## Thomas Love Peacock
### *The War-Song of Dinas Vawr*

The mountain sheep are sweeter,
But the valley sheep are fatter;
We therefore deemed it meeter
To carry off the latter.
5  We made an expedition;
We met a host and quelled it;
We forced a strong position
And killed the men who held it.

On Dyfed's° richest valley,          *Kingdom in ancient Wales*
10  Where herds of kine were browsing,
We made a mighty sally,
To furnish our carousing.
Fierce warriors rushed to meet us;
We met them, and o'erthrew them:
15  They struggled hard to beat us,
But we conquered them and slew them.

As we drove our prize at leisure,
The king marched forth to catch us:
His rage surpassed all measure,
20  But his people could not match us.
He fled to his hall-pillars;
And, ere our force we led off,

93

Some sacked his house and cellars,
While others cut his head off.

25 We there, in strife bewild'ring,
Spilt blood enough to swim in:
We orphaned many children
And widowed many women.
The eagles and the ravens
30 We glutted with our foemen;
The heroes and the cravens,
The spearmen and the bowmen.

We brought away from battle,
And much their land bemoaned them,
35 Two thousand head of cattle
And the head of him who owned them:
Ednyfed, king of Dyfed,
His head was borne before us;
His wine and beasts supplied our feasts
40 And his overthrow, our chorus.

BERTRAN DE BORN
*How I Like the Gay Time of Spring**

How I like the gay time of spring
That makes leaves and flowers grow,
And how I like the piercing ring
Of birds, as their songs go
5        Echoing among the woods.
I like it when I see the yield
Of tents and pavilions in fields,
        And O, it makes me feel good
To see arrayed on battlefields
10 Horses and horsemen with shields.

And I like it when the scouts
Make people with property flee
And I like it when I see the rout
Of a swarm of opposing armies,
15        And O, how my spirits adore
The sight of strong castles attacked

* Translated by James J. Wilhelm

*94*

With barricades broken and hacked
 And troops waiting on the shore
That's completely encircled by ditches
20 With strong-staked rows interstitched.

And likewise I like a lord
Who's the first man in the fray
On horse, armed, fearlessly forward,
Inspiring his men to obey
25  With valiant deeds;
And when the battle's fierce
Everyone's prompt to pierce
 And freely follow his lead,
For a soldier's soon forsaken
30 Till he's given many blows—and taken.

Maces, swords, helmets—colorfully—
Shields, slicing and smashing,
We'll see at the start of the melee
With all those vassals clashing
35  And horses running free
From their masters, hit, downtread.
Once the charge is led
 Every man of nobility
Will hack at arms and heads.
40 Better than be taken prisoner: to be dead.

I tell you: no pleasure's so large
(Not eating or drinking or sleep)
As when I hear the cry: "Charge!"
Or out of the darkened deep
45  A horse's whinnying refrain,
Or the cry: "Help! Bring aid!"
As big and little cascade
 Into ditches across the plain,
And I see, by the corpses whose sides
50 Are splintered, flags furling wide.

Barons, put up your bets:
Those castles, cities, lands you adore
Before you start bringing *us* war!

*Disabled*

He sat in a wheeled chair, waiting for dark,
And shivered in his ghastly suit of gray,
Legless, sewn short at elbow. Through the park
Voices of boys rang saddening like a hymn,
5   Voices of play and pleasures after day,
Till gathering sleep had mothered them from him.

About this time Town used to swing so gay
When glow-lamps budded in the light blue trees,
And girls glanced lovelier as the air grew dim,—
10  In the old times, before he threw away his knees.
Now he will never feel again how slim
Girls' waists are, or how warm their subtle hands;
All of them touch him like some queer disease.

There was an artist silly for his face,
15  For it was younger than his youth, last year.
Now, he is old; his back will never brace;
He's lost his color very far from here,
Poured it down shell-holes till the veins ran dry,
And half his lifetime lapsed in the hot race,
20  And leap of purple spurted from his thigh.

One time he liked a blood-smear down his leg,
After the matches, carried shoulder-high.
It was after football, when he'd drunk a peg,
He thought he'd better join.—He wonders why.
25  Someone had said he'd look a god in kilts,
That's why; and may be, too, to please his Meg;
Aye, that was it, to please the giddy jilts
He asked to join. He didn't have to beg;

Smiling they wrote his lie; aged nineteen years.
30  Germans he scarcely thought of; all their guilt,
And Austria's, did not move him. And no fears
Of Fear came yet. He thought of jeweled hilts
For daggers in plaid socks; of smart salutes;
And care of arms; and leave; and pay arrears;
35  *Esprit de corps*, and hints for young recruits.
And soon he was drafted out with drums and cheers.

Some cheered him home, but not as crowds cheer Goal.
Only a solemn man who brought him fruits
*Thanked* him; and then inquired about his soul.

40  Now, he will spend a few sick years in Institutes,
And do what things the rules consider wise,
And take whatever pity they may dole.
Tonight he noticed how the women's eyes
Passed from him to the strong men that were whole.
45  How cold and late it is! Why don't they come
And put him into bed? Why don't they come?


ANONYMOUS
## Johnny, I Hardly Knew Ye
*Irish popular ballad; eighteenth century*

While going the road to sweet Athy,
    Hurroo! Hurroo!
While going the road to sweet Athy,
    Hurroo! Hurroo!
5  While going the road to sweet Athy,
A stick in my hand and a drop in my eye,
A doleful damsel I heard cry:
    "Och, Johnny, I hardly knew ye!

(*Chorus:*)

" *With drums and guns, and guns and drums*
10    *The enemy near slew ye;*
*My darling dear, you look so queer,*
    *Och, Johnny, I hardly knew ye!*

"Where are your eyes that looked so mild?
    Hurroo! Hurroo!
15  Where are your eyes that looked so mild
When my poor heart you first beguiled?
Why did you run from me and the child?
    Och, Johnny, I hardly knew ye!

"Where are the legs with which you run?
20    Hurroo! Hurroo!
Where are the legs with which you run
When you went off to carry a gun?—
Indeed your dancing days are done!
    Och, Johnny, I hardly knew ye!

25   "It grieved my heart to see you sail,
     Hurroo! Hurroo!
  It grieved my heart to see you sail
  Though from my heart you took leg bail°         *Took flight*
  Like a cod you're doubled up head and tail,
30      Och, Johnny, I hardly knew ye!

  "You haven't an arm and you haven't a leg,
     Hurroo! Hurroo!
  You haven't an arm and you haven't a leg,
  You're an eyeless, noseless, chickenless egg,
35   You'll have to be put in a bowl to beg,
     Och, Johnny, I hardly knew ye!

  "It's happy I am for to see you home,
     Hurroo! Hurroo!
  It's happy I am for to see you home,
40   All from the island of Sulloon,
  So low in flesh, so high in bone,
     Och, Johnny, I hardly knew ye!

  "But sad as it is to see you so,
     Hurroo! Hurroo!
45   But sad as it is to see you so,
  And to think of you now as an object of woe,
  Your Peggy'll still keep ye on as her beau—
     Och, Johnny, I hardly knew ye!"

# Section V

## Sir Walter Raleigh
### What Is Our Life?

What is our life? a play of passion;
Our mirth, the music of division,°     *Music between acts of a play*
Our mothers' wombs the tiring-houses be
Where we are dressed for this short comedy.
5   Heaven the judicious sharp spectator is,
That sits and marks still who doth act amiss;
Our graves that hide us from the searching sun
Are like drawn curtains when the play is done.
Thus march we playing to our latest rest;
10  Only we die in earnest—that's no jest.


## William Shakespeare
### All the World's a Stage
*From* As You Like It

All the world's a stage
And all the men and women merely players:
They have their exits and their entrances;
And one man in his time plays many parts,
5   His acts being seven ages. At first the infant,
Mewling and puking in the nurse's arms.
Then the whining school-boy, with his satchel
And shining morning face, creeping like snail
Unwillingly to school. And then the lover,
10  Sighing like a furnace, with a woeful ballad
Made to his mistress' eyebrow. Then a soldier,
Full of strange oaths, and bearded like the pard,°     *Leopard*
Jealous in honor, sudden and quick in quarrel,
Seeking the bubble reputation
15  Even in the cannon's mouth. And then the justice,
In fair round belly with good capon° lined,     *A castrated rooster*
With eyes severe and beard of formal cut,
Full of wise saws and modern instances;
And so he plays his part. The sixth age shifts
20  Into the lean and slipper'd pantaloon,
With spectacles on nose and pouch on side,
His youthful hose, well saved, a world too wide
For his shrunk shank; and his big manly voice,
Turning again toward childish treble, pipes

25 And whistles in his sound. Last scene of all,
   That ends this strange eventful history,
Is second childishness and mere oblivion,
Sans° teeth, sans eyes, sans taste, sans every thing.      *Without*

EDGAR ALLAN POE
*The Conqueror Worm*

    Lo! 'tis a gala night
      Within the lonesome latter years!
    An angel throng, bewinged, bedight
      In veils, and drowned in tears,
5   Sit in a theatre, to see
      A play of hopes and fears,
    While the orchestra breathes fitfully
      The music of the spheres.

    Mimes, in the form of God on high,
10     Mutter and mumble low,
    And hither and thither fly—
      Mere puppets they, who come and go
    At bidding of vast formless things
      That shift the scenery to and fro,
15 Flapping from out their Condor wings
      Invisible Wo!

    That motley drama—oh, be sure
      It shall not be forgot!
    With its Phantom chased for evermore
20     By a crowd that seize it not,
    Through a circle that ever returneth in
      To the self-same spot,
    And much of Madness, and more of Sin,
      And Horror the soul of the plot.

25 But see, amid the mimic rout,
      A crawling shape intrude!
    A blood-red thing that writhes from out
      The scenic solitude!
    It writhes!—it writhes!—with mortal pangs
30     The mimes become its food,
    And seraphs sob at vermin fangs
      In human gore imbued.

Out—out are the lights—out all!
    And, over each quivering form,
35  The curtain, a funeral pall,
    Comes down with the rush of a storm,
While the angels, all pallid and wan,
    Uprising, unveiling, affirm
That the play is the tragedy, "Man,"
40      And its hero, the Conqueror Worm.

HENRY VAUGHAN
*They Are All Gone into the World of Light!*

They are all gone into the world of light!
    And I alone sit lingering here;
Their very memory is fair and bright,
    And my sad thoughts doth clear.

5   It glows and glitters in my cloudy breast
    Like stars upon some gloomy grove,
Or those faint beams in which this hill is dressed
    After the sun's remove.

I see them walking in an air of glory,
10      Whose light doth trample on my days;
My days, which are at best but dull and hoary,
    Mere glimmering and decays.

O holy hope, and high humility,
    High as the heavens above!
15  These are your walks, and you have showed them me
    To kindle my cold love.

Dear, beauteous death! the jewel of the just,
    Shining nowhere but in the dark;
What mysteries do lie beyond thy dust,
20      Could man outlook that mark!°                    *Boundary*

He that hath found some fledged bird's nest may know
    At first sight if the bird be flown;
But what fair well or grove he sings in now,
    That is to him unknown.

103

25 And yet, as angels in some brighter dreams
    Call to the soul when man doth sleep,
So some strange thoughts transcend our wonted themes,
    And into glory peep.

If a star were confined into a tomb,
30    Her captive flames must needs burn there;
But when the hand that locked her up gives room,
    She'll shine through all the sphere.

O Father of eternal life, and all
    Created glories under Thee!
35 Resume° Thy spirit from this world of thrall          *Take back*
    Into true liberty!

Either disperse these mists, which blot and fill
    My perspective° still as they pass;                 *Telescope*
Or else remove me hence unto that hill
40    Where I shall need no glass.


WILLIAM WORDSWORTH
*Ode*
Intimations of Immortality from Recollections of Early
Childhood

> *The Child is father of the Man;*
> *And I could wish my days to be*
> *Bound each to each by natural piety.*


1

There was a time when meadow, grove, and stream,
The earth, and every common sight,
        To me did seem
        Appareled in celestial light,
5 The glory and the freshness of a dream.
It is not now as it hath been of yore—
        Turn whereso'er I may,
        By night or day,
The things which I have seen I now can see no more.


2

10        The Rainbow comes and goes,
        And lovely is the Rose,

The Moon doth with delight
Look round her when the heavens are bare,
Waters on a starry night
15     Are beautiful and fair;
The sunshine is a glorious birth;
But yet I know, where'er I go,
That there hath passed away a glory from the earth.


### 3

Now, while the birds thus sing a joyous song,
20   And while the young lambs bound
    As to the tabor's° sound,            *Small drum*
To me alone there came a thought of grief:
A timely utterance gave that thought relief,
    And I again am strong:
25 The cataracts blow their trumpets from the steep;
No more shall grief of mine the season wrong;
I hear the Echoes through the mountains throng,
The Winds come to me from the fields of sleep,
    And all the earth is gay;
30       Land and sea
  Give themselves up to jollity,
    And with the heart of May
  Doth every Beast keep holiday—
    Thou Child of Joy,
35 Shout round me, let me hear thy shouts, thou happy Shepherd-
  boy!

### 4

Ye blessèd Creatures, I have heard the call
  Ye to each other make; I see
The heavens laugh with you in your jubilee;
  My heart is at your festival,
40   My head hath its coronal,
The fullness of your bliss, I feel—I feel it all.
    Oh, evil day! if I were sullen
    While Earth herself is adorning,
      This sweet May morning,
45     And the Children are culling
      On every side,
    In a thousand valleys far and wide,
    Fresh flowers; while the sun shines warm,
And the Babe leaps up on his Mother's arm—
50     I hear, I hear, with joy I hear!

—But there's a Tree, of many, one,
A single Field which I have looked upon,
Both of them speak of something that is gone:
  The Pansy at my feet
55    Doth the same tale repeat:
Whither is fled the visionary gleam?
Where is it now, the glory and the dream?


### 5

Our birth is but a sleep and a forgetting:
The Soul that rises with us, our life's Star,
60   Hath had elsewhere its setting,
   And cometh from afar:
  Not in entire forgetfulness,
  And not in utter nakedness,
But trailing clouds of glory do we come
65   From God, who is our home:
Heaven lies about us in our infancy!
Shades of the prison-house begin to close
  Upon the growing Boy
   But he
70 Beholds the light, and whence it flows,
  He sees it in his joy;
The Youth, who daily farther from the east
  Must travel, still is Nature's Priest,
  And by the vision splendid
75   Is on his way attended;
At length the Man perceives it die away,
And fade into the light of common day.


### 6

Earth fills her lap with pleasures of her own;
Yearnings she hath in her own natural kind,
80 And, even with something of a Mother's mind,
  And no unworthy aim,
  The homely° Nurse doth all she can     *Simple or kindly*
To make her foster child, her Inmate Man,
  Forget the glories he hath known,
85 And that imperial palace whence he came.


### 7

Behold the Child among his newborn blisses,
A six-years' Darling of a pygmy size!

See, where 'mid work of his own hand he lies,
Fretted by sallies of his mother's kisses,
90  With light upon him from his father's eyes!
See, at his feet, some little plan or chart,
Some fragment from his dream of human life,
Shaped by himself with newly-learnéd art;
        A wedding or a festival,
95        A mourning or a funeral;
          And this hath now his heart,
          And unto this he frames his song;
            Then will he fit his tongue
To dialogues of business, love, or strife;
100        But it will not be long
          Ere this be thrown aside,
          And with new joy and pride
The little Actor cons another part;
Filling from time to time his "humorous stage"°        *Refers to*
105  With all the Persons, down to palsied Age,          *Elizabethan*
That Life brings with her in her equipage;            *humors; states of*
        As if his whole vocation                       *mind; temperament*
        Were endless imitation.

                    *8*

Thou, whose exterior semblance doth belie
110        Thy Soul's immensity;
Thou best Philosopher, who yet dost keep
Thy heritage, thou Eye among the blind,
That, deaf and silent, read'st the eternal deep,
Haunted forever by the eternal mind—
115        Mighty Prophet! Seer blest!
          On whom those truths do rest,
Which we are toiling all our lives to find,
In darkness lost, the darkness of the grave;
Thou, over whom thy Immortality
120  Broods like the Day, a Master o'er a Slave,
A Presence which is not to be put by;
Thou little Child, yet glorious in the might
Of heaven-born freedom on thy being's height,
Why with such earnest pains dost thou provoke
125  The years to bring the inevitable yoke,
Thus blindly with thy blessedness at strife?
Full soon thy Soul shall have her earthly freight,
And custom lie upon thee with a weight,
Heavy as frost, and deep almost as life!

## 9

130         O joy! that in our embers
            Is something that doth live,
            That nature yet remembers
            What was so fugitive!
   The thought of our past years in me doth breed
135 Perpetual benediction: not indeed
For that which is most worthy to be blest;
Delight and liberty, the simple creed
Of Childhood, whether busy or at rest,
With new-fledged hope still fluttering in his breast—
140         Not for these I raise
          The song of thanks and praise;
      But for those obstinate questionings
      Of sense and outward things,
      Fallings from us, vanishings;
145       Blank misgivings of a Creature
Moving about in worlds not realized,
High instincts before which our mortal Nature
Did tremble like a guilty Thing surprised;
      But for those first affections,
150       Those shadowy recollections,
       Which, be they what they may,
Are yet the fountain light of all our day,
Are yet a master light of all our seeing;
      Uphold us, cherish, and have power to make
155 Our noisy years seem moments in the being
Of the eternal Silence: truths that wake,
         To perish never;
Which neither listlessness, nor mad endeavor,
        Nor Man nor Boy,
160 Nor all that is at enmity with joy,
Can utterly abolish or destroy!
        Hence in a season of calm weather
        Though inland far we be,
Our Souls have sight of that immortal sea
165         Which brought us hither,
        Can in a moment travel thither,
And see the Children sport upon the shore,
And hear the mighty waters rolling evermore.

*10*

Then sing, ye Birds, sing, sing a joyous song!
170       And let the young Lambs bound

As to the tabor's sound!
We in thought will join your throng,
    Ye that pipe and ye that play,
    Ye that through your hearts today
175        Feel the gladness of the May!
What though the radiance which was once so bright
Be now forever taken from my sight,
    Though nothing can bring back the hour
Of splendor in the grass, of glory in the flower;
180        We will grieve not, rather find
    Strength in what remains behind;
    In the primal sympathy
    Which having been must ever be;
    In the soothing thoughts that spring
185        Out of human suffering;
    In the faith that looks through death,
In years that bring the philosophic mind.

### 11

And O, ye Fountains, Meadows, Hills, and Groves,
Forebode not any severing of our loves!
190 Yet in my heart of hearts I feel your might;
I only have relinquished one delight
To live beneath your more habitual sway.
I love the Brooks which down their channels fret,
Even more than when I tripped lightly as they;
195 The innocent brightness of a newborn Day
        Is lovely yet;
The clouds that gather round the setting sun
Do take a sober coloring from an eye
That hath kept watch o'er man's mortality;
200 Another race hath been, and other palms° are won.          *Symbols of*
Thanks to the human heart by which we live,                          *victory*
Thanks to its tenderness, its joys, and fears,
To me the meanest° flower that blows° can give                    *Simplest*
Thoughts that do often lie too deep for tears.                        *Blooms*

## John Donne
### *Batter My Heart*
*From* Holy Sonnets

### XIV

Batter my heart, three personed God; for you
As yet but knock, breathe, shine, and seek to mend;
That I may rise and stand, o'erthrow me and bend
Your force to break, blow, burn and make me new.
5   I, like an usurped town, to another due,
Labour to admit you, but oh, to no end;
Reason, your viceroy in me, me should defend,
But is captived and proves weak or untrue.
Yet dearly I love you and would be loved fain,
10   But am betrothed unto your enemy:
Divorce me, untie or break that knot again,
Take me to you, imprison me, for I
Except you enthrall me, never shall be free,
Nor ever chaste, except you ravish me.

## Carl Sandburg
### *Prayers of Steel*

Lay me on an anvil, O God.
Beat me and hammer me into a crowbar.
Let me pry loose old walls;
Let me lift and loosen old foundations.

5   Lay me on an anvil, O God.
Beat me and hammer me into a steel spike.
Drive me into the girders that hold a skyscraper together.
Take red-hot rivets and fasten me into the central girders.
Let me be the great nail holding a skyscraper through blue nights
    into white stars.

# George Gordon, Lord Byron
## *I Would I Were a Careless Child*

### 1

I would I were a careless child,
    Still dwelling in my Highland cave,
Or roaming through the dusky wild,
    Or bounding o'er the dark blue wave;
5 The cumbrous pomp of Saxon pride,
    Accords not with the freeborn soul,
Which loves the mountain's craggy side,
    And seeks the rocks where billows roll.

### 2

Fortune! take back these cultur'd lands,
10     Take back this name of splendid sound!
I hate the touch of servile hands,
    I hate the slaves that cringe around:
Place me among the rocks I love,
    Which sound to Ocean's wildest roar;
15 I ask but this—again to rove
    Through scenes my youth hath known before.

### 3

Few are my years, and yet I feel
    The World was ne'er design'd for me:
Ah! why do dark'ning shades conceal
20     The hour when man must cease to be?
Once I beheld a splendid dream,
    A visionary scene of bliss:
Truth!—wherefore did thy hated beam
    Awake me to a world like this?

### 4

25 I lov'd—but those I lov'd are gone;
    Had friends—my early friends are fled.
How cheerless feels the heart alone,
    When all its former hopes are dead!
Though gay companions, o'er the bowl
30     Dispel awhile the sense of ill;
Though Pleasure stirs the maddening soul,
    The heart—the heart—is lonely still.

How dull! to hear the voice of those
    Whom Rank or Chance, whom Wealth or Power,
35  Have made, though neither friends nor foes,
    Associates of the festive hour.
Give me again a faithful few,
    In years and feelings still the same,
And I will fly the midnight crew,
40    Where boist'rous Joy is but a name.

6

And Woman, lovely Woman! thou,
    My hope, my comforter, my all!
How cold must be my bosom now,
    When e'en thy smiles begin to pall!
45  Without a sigh would I resign,
    This busy scene of splendid Woe,
To make that calm contentment mine,
    Which Virtue knows, or seems to know.

7

Fain would I fly the haunts of men—
50    I seek to shun, not hate mankind;
My breast requires the sullen glen,
    Whose gloom may suit a darken'd mind.
Oh! that to me the wings were given,
    Which bear the turtle° to her nest!        *Turtle dove*
55  Then would I cleave the vault of Heaven,
    To flee away, and be at rest.

DYLAN THOMAS
*Fern Hill*

Now as I was young and easy under the apple boughs
About the lilting house and happy as the grass was green,
    The night above the dingle° starry,      *Small, deep,*
      Time let me hail and climb      *wooded valley*
5      Golden in the heydays of his eyes,
And honored among wagons I was prince of the apple towns
And once below a time I lordly had the trees and leaves
      Trail with daisies and barley
    Down the rivers of the windfall light.

10 And as I was green and carefree, famous among the barns
About the happy yard and singing as the farm was home,
In the sun that is young once only,
Time let me play and be
Golden in the mercy of his means,
15 And green and golden I was huntsman and herdsman, the calves
Sang to my horn, the foxes on the hills barked clear and cold,
And the sabbath rang slowly
In the pebbles of the holy streams.

All the sun long it was running, it was lovely, the hay
20 Fields high as the house, the tunes from the chimneys, it was air
And playing, lovely and watery
And fire green as grass.
And nightly under the simple stars
As I rode to sleep the owls were bearing the farm away,
25 All the moon long I heard, blessed among stables, the night-jars
Flying with the ricks, and the horses
Flashing into the dark.

And then to awake, and the farm, like a wanderer white
With the dew, come back, the cock on his shoulder: it was all
30 Shining, it was Adam and maiden,
The sky gathered again
And the sun grew round that very day.
So it must have been after the birth of the simple light
In the first, spinning place, the spellbound horses walking warm
35 Out of the whinnying green stable
On to the fields of praise.

And honored among foxes and pheasants by the gay house
Under the new made clouds and happy as the heart was long,
In the sun born over and over,
40 I ran my heedless ways,
My wishes raced through the house high hay
And nothing I cared, at my sky blue trades, that time allows
In all his tuneful turning so few and such morning songs
Before the children green and golden
45 Follow him out of grace,

Nothing I cared, in the lamb white days, that time would take me
Up to the swallow thronged loft by the shadow of my hand,
In the moon that is always rising,
Nor that riding to sleep

*113*

I should hear him fly with the high fields
And wake to the farm forever fled from the childless land.
Oh as I as young and easy in the mercy of his means,
          Time held me green and dying
     Though I sang in my chains like the sea.

SAMUEL TAYLOR COLERIDGE
*Frost at Midnight*

     The Frost performs its secret ministry,
     Unhelped by any wind. The owlet's cry
     Came loud—and hark, again! loud as before.
     The inmates of my cottage, all at rest,
5    Have left me to that solitude, which suits
     Abstruser musings: save that at my side
     My cradled infant slumbers peacefully.
     'Tis calm indeed! so calm, that it disturbs
     And vexes meditation with its strange
10   And extreme silentness. Sea, hill, and wood,
     This populous village! Sea, and hill, and wood,
     With all the numberless goings-on of life,
     Inaudible as dreams! the thin blue flame
     Lies on my low-burnt fire, and quivers not;
15   Only that film, which fluttered on the grate,
     Still flutters there, the sole unquiet thing.
     Methinks its motion in this hush of nature
     Gives it dim sympathies with me who live,
     Making it a companionable form,
20   Whose puny flaps and freaks the idling Spirit
     By its own moods interprets, everywhere
     Echo or mirror seeking of itself,
     And makes a toy of Thought.
                         But O! how oft,
     How oft, at school, with most believing mind,
25   Presageful,° have I gazed upon the bars,                    *Foretelling*
     To watch that fluttering *stranger!* and as oft
     With unclosed lids, already had I dreamt
     Of my sweet birthplace, and the old church tower,
     Whose bells, the poor man's only music, rang
30   From morn to evening, all the hot Fair-day,°               *Market day*

*114*

So sweetly, that they stirred and haunted me
With a wild pleasure, falling on mine ear
Most like articulate sounds of things to come!
So gazed I, till the soothing things, I dreamt,
35 Lulled me to sleep, and sleep prolonged my dreams!
And so I brooded all the following morn,
Awed by the stern preceptor's° face, mine eye          *Schoolmaster's*
Fixed with mock study on my swimming book:
Save if the door half opened, and I snatched
40 A hasty glance, and still my heart leaped up,
For still I hoped to see the *stranger's* face,
Townsman, or aunt, or sister more beloved,
My playmate when we both were clothed alike!°          *In early*
                                                        *childhood, when*
    Dear Babe, that sleepest cradled by my side,        *boys and girls*
45 Whose gentle breathings, heard in this deep calm,        *wore the*
Fill up the interspersèd vacancies                *same kind of infants'*
And momentary pauses of the thought!                    *clothing*
My babe so beautiful! it thrills my heart
With tender gladness, thus to look at thee,
50 And think that thou shalt learn far other lore,
And in far other scenes! For I was reared
In the great city, pent 'mid cloisters dim,
And saw nought lovely but the sky and stars.
But thou, my babe! shalt wander like a breeze
55 By lakes and sandy shores, beneath the crags
Of ancient mountain, and beneath the clouds,
Which image in their bulk both lakes and shores
And mountain crags: so shalt thou see and hear
The lovely shapes and sounds intelligible
60 Of that eternal language, which thy God
Utters, who from eternity doth teach
Himself in all, and all things in himself.
Great universal Teacher! he shall mold
Thy spirit, and by giving make it ask.

65     Therefore all seasons shall be sweet to thee,
Whether the summer clothe the general° earth          *Generative,*
With greenness, or the redbreast sit and sing            *vernal*
Betwixt the tufts of snow on the bare branch
Of mossy apple tree, while the nigh thatch
70 Smokes in the sun-thaw; whether the eave-drops fall
Heard only in the trances of the blast,
Or if the secret ministry of frost

Shall hang them up in silent icicles,
Quietly shining to the quiet Moon.


WALT WHITMAN
*There Was a Child Went Forth*

There was a child went forth every day,
And the first object he look'd upon, that object he became,
And that object became part of him for the day or a certain part of
    the day,
Or for many years or stretching cycles of years.

5   The early lilacs became part of this child,
And grass and white and red morning-glories, and white and red
    clover, and the song of the phœbe-bird,
And the Third-month lambs, and the sow's pink-faint litter, and
    the mare's foal and the cow's calf,
And the noisy brood of the barnyard or by the mire of the pond-
    side,
And the fish suspending themselves so curiously below there, and
    the beautiful curious liquid,
10  And the water-plants with their graceful flat heads, all became
    part of him.

The field-sprouts of Fourth-month and Fifth-month became part
    of him,
Winter-grain sprouts and those of the light-yellow corn, and the
    esculent roots of the garden,
And the apple-trees cover'd with blossoms and the fruit afterward,
    and wood-berries, and the commonest weeds by the road,
And the old drunkard staggering home from the outhouse of the
    tavern whence he had lately risen,
15  And the schoolmistress that pass'd on her way to the school,
And the friendly boys that pass'd, and the quarrelsome boys,
And the tidy and fresh-cheek'd girls, and the barefoot negro boy
    and girl,
And all the changes of city and country wherever he went.

His own parents, he that had father'd him and she that had con-
    ceiv'd him in her womb and birth'd him,
20  They gave this child more of themselves than that,
They gave him afterward every day, they became part of him.

The mother at home quietly placing the dishes on the supper-table,
The mother with mild words, clean her cap and gown, a whole-
    some odor falling off her person and clothes as she walks by,
The father, strong, self-sufficient, manly, mean, anger'd, unjust,
25  The blow, the quick loud word, the tight bargain, the crafty lure,
The family usages, the language, the company, the furniture, the
    yearning and swelling heart,
Affection that will not be gainsay'd, the sense of what is real, the
    thought if after all it should prove unreal,
The doubts of day-time and the doubts of night-time, the curious
    whether and how,
Whether that which appears so is so, or is it all flashes and specks?
30  Men and women crowding fast in the streets, if they are not
    flashes and specks what are they?
The streets themselves and the façades of houses, and goods in the
    windows,
Vehicles, teams, the heavy-plank'd wharves, the huge crossing at
    the ferries,
The village on the highland seen from afar at sunset; the river
    between,
Shadows, aureola and mist, the light falling on roofs and gables
    of white or brown two miles off,
35  The schooner near by sleepily dropping down the tide, the little
    boat slack-tow'd astern,
The hurrying tumbling waves, quick-broken crests, slapping,
The strata of color'd clouds, the long bar of maroon-tint away
    solitary by itself, the spread of purity it lies motionless in,
The horizon's edge, the flying sea-crow, the fragrance of salt
    marsh and shore mud,
These became part of that child who went forth every day, and
    who now goes, and will always go forth every day.

EMILY BRONTË
*No Coward Soul Is Mine*

No coward soul is mine,
No trembler in the world's storm-troubled sphere;
    I see Heaven's glories shine,
And faith shines equal, arming me from fear.

5    O God within my breast,
Almighty ever-present Deity!
      Life—that in me has rest,
As I—undying Life—have power in Thee!

      Vain are the thousand creeds
10   That move men's hearts—unutterably vain;
      Worthless as withered weeds,
Or idlest froth amid the boundless main,

      To waken doubt in one
Holding so fast by Thine infinity;
15      So surely anchored on
The steadfast rock of immortality.

      With wide-embracing love
Thy spirit animates eternal years
      Pervades and broods above,
20   Changes, sustains, dissolves, creates, and rears.

      Though earth and man were gone,
And suns and universes ceased to be,
      And Thou were left alone,
Every existence would exist in Thee.

25   There is not room for Death,
Nor atom that his might could render void;
      Thou—Thou art Being and Breath,
And what Thou art may never be destroyed.


WILLIAM ERNEST HENLEY
*Invictus*

      Out of the night that covers me,
         Black as the Pit from pole to pole,
      I thank whatever gods may be
         For my unconquerable soul.

5    In the fell clutch of circumstance
         I have not winced nor cried aloud.
      Under the bludgeonings of chance
         My head is bloody, but unbowed.

Beyond this place of wrath and tears
10      Looms but the horror of the shade,
And yet the menace of the years
    Finds, and shall find me, unafraid.

It matters not how strait the gate,
    How charged with punishments the scroll,
15  I am the master of my fate:
    I am the captain of my soul.

THOMAS HARDY
*Waiting Both*

    A star looks down at me,
    And says: "Here I and you
    Stand, each in our degree:
    What do you mean to do—
5       Mean to do?"

    I say: "For all I know,
    Wait, and let Time go by,
    Till my change come."—"Just so,"
    The star says: "So mean I—
10      So mean I."

STEPHEN CRANE
*A Man Said to the Universe*

    A man said to the universe:
    "Sir, I exist!"
    "However," replied the universe,
    "The fact has not created in me
5   A sense of obligation."

*View of a Pig*

The pig lay on a barrow dead.
It weighed, they said, as much as three men.
Its eyes closed, pink white eyelashes.
Its trotters stuck straight out.

5   Such weight and thick pink bulk
Set in death seemed not just dead.
It was less than lifeless, further off.
It was like a sack of wheat.

I thumped it without feeling remorse.
10  One feels guilty insulting the dead,
Walking on graves. But this pig
Did not seem able to accuse.

It was too dead. Just so much
A poundage of lard and pork.
15  Its last dignity had entirely gone.
It was not a figure of fun.

Too dead now to pity.
To remember its life, din, stronghold
Of earthly pleasure as it had been,
20  Seemed a false effort, and off the point.

Too deadly factual. Its weight
Oppressed me—how could it be moved?
And the trouble of cutting it up!
The gash in its throat was shocking, but not pathetic.

25  Once I ran at a fair in the noise
To catch a greased piglet
That was faster and nimbler than a cat,
Its squeal was the rending of metal.

Pigs must have hot blood, they feel like ovens.
30  Their bite is worse than a horse's—
They chop a half-moon clean out.
They eat cinders, dead cats.

Distinctions and admirations such
As this one was long finished with.
35  I stared at it a long time. They were going to scald it,
Scald it and scour it like a doorstep.

IRVING LAYTON
*The Bull Calf*

The thing could barely stand. Yet taken
from his mother and the barn smells
he still impressed with his pride,
with the promise of sovereignty in the way
5   his head moved to take us in.
The fierce sunlight tugging the maize from the ground
licked at his shapely flanks.
He was too young for all that pride.
I thought of the deposed Richard II.

10  "No money in bull calves," Freeman had said.
The visiting clergyman rubbed the nostrils
now snuffing pathetically at the windless day.
"A pity," he sighed.
My gaze slipped off his hat toward the empty sky
15  that circled over the black knot of men,
over us and the calf waiting for the first blow.

Struck,
the bull calf drew in his thin forelegs
as if gathering strength for a mad rush . . .
20  tottered . . . raised his darkening eyes to us,
and I saw we were at the far end
of his frightened look, growing smaller and smaller
till we were only the ponderous mallet
that flicked his bleeding ear
25  and pushed him over on his side, stiffly,
like a block of wood.

Below the hill's crest
the river snuffled on the improvised beach.
We dug a deep pit and threw the dead calf into it.
30  It made a wet sound, a sepulchral gurgle,
as the warm sides bulged and flattened.
Settled, the bull calf lay as if asleep,
one foreleg over the other,
bereft of pride and so beautiful now,
35  without movement, perfectly still in the cool pit,
I turned away and wept.

# JOHN CLARE
## *Badger*

When midnight comes a host of dogs and men
Go out and track the badger to his den,
And put a sack within the hole, and lie
Till the old grunting badger passes by.
5  He comes and hears—they let the strongest loose.
The old fox hears the noise and drops the goose.
The poacher shoots and hurries from the cry,
And the old hare half wounded buzzes by.
They get a forkéd stick to bear him down
10  And clap the dogs and take him to the town,
And bait him all the day with many dogs,
And laugh and shout and fright the scampering hogs.
He runs along and bites at all he meets:
They shout and hollo down the noisy streets.

15  He turns about to face the loud uproar
And drives the rebels to their very door.
The frequent stone is hurled where'er they go;
When badgers fight, then everyone's a foe.
The dogs are clapped and urged to join the fray;
20  The badger turns and drives them all away.
Though scarcely half as big, demure and small,
He fights with dogs for hours and beats them all.
The heavy mastiff, savage in the fray,
Lies down and licks his feet and turns away.
25  The bulldog knows his match and waxes cold,
The badger grins and never leaves his hold.
He drives the crowd and follows at their heels
And bites them through—the drunkard swears and reels.

The frighted women take the boys away,
30  The blackguard laughs and hurries on the fray.
He tries to reach the woods, an awkward race,
But sticks and cudgels quickly stop the chase.
He turns again and drives the noisy crowd
And beats the many dogs in noises loud.
35  He drives away and beats them every one,
And then they loose them all and set them on.
He falls as dead and kicked by boys and men,
Then starts and grins and drives the crowd again;
Till kicked and torn and beaten out he lies
40  And leaves his hold and crackles, groans, and dies.

# Section VI

# WILLIAM WORDSWORTH
## *Mutability*

From low to high doth dissolution climb,
And sink from high to low, along a scale
Of awful notes, whose concord shall not fail;
A musical but melancholy chime,
5   Which they can hear who meddle not with crime,
Nor avarice, nor over-anxious care.
Truth fails not; but her outward forms that bear
The longest date do melt like frosty rime,°        *Thin coating*
That in the morning whitened hill and plain
10  And is no more; drop like the tower sublime
Of yesterday, which royally did wear
His crown of weeds, but could not even sustain
Some casual shout that broke the silent air,
Or the unimaginable touch of Time.

# PERCY BYSSHE SHELLEY
## *Mutability*

### 1

The flower that smiles today
     Tomorrow dies;
All that we wish to stay,
     Tempts and then flies.
5   What is this world's delight?
Lightning that mocks the night,
  Brief even as bright.

### 2

Virtue, how frail it is!
     Friendship how rare!
10  Love, how it sells poor bliss
     For proud despair!
But we, though soon they fall,
Survive their joy and all
  Which ours we call.

### 3

15  Whilst skies are blue and bright,
     Whilst flowers are gay,

Whilst eyes that change ere night
    Make glad the day,
Whilst yet the calm hours creep,
20  Dream thou—and from thy sleep
    Then wake to weep.

## WALTER SAVAGE LANDOR
*On Seeing a Hair of Lucretia Borgia*

Borgia, thou once wert almost too august
And high for adoration—now thou'rt dust;
All that remains of thee these plaits infold,
Calm hair, meandering with pellucid° gold!       *Transparent*

## E. E. CUMMINGS
*Buffalo Bill's Defunct*

Buffalo Bill's
defunct
       who used to
       ride a watersmooth-silver
5                             stallion
and break onetwothreefourfive pigeonsjustlikethat
                                     Jesus
he was a handsome man
                     and what i want to know is

10  how do you like your blueeyed boy
Mister Death

## ARCHIBALD MACLEISH
*The End of the World*

Quite unexpectedly as Vasserot
The armless ambidextrian was lighting

A match between his great and second toe
And Ralph the lion was engaged in biting
5  The neck of Madame Sossman while the drum
Pointed, and Teeny was about to cough
In waltz-time swinging Jocko by the thumb—
Quite unexpectedly the top blew off:
And there, there overhead, there, there, hung over
10  Those thousands of white faces, those dazed eyes,
There in the starless dark the poise, the hover,
There with vast wings across the canceled skies,
There in the sudden blackness the black pall
Of nothing, nothing, nothing—nothing at all.


ROBERT FROST
*Fire and Ice*

Some say the world will end in fire,
Some say in ice.
From what I've tasted of desire
I hold with those who favor fire.
5  But if it had to perish twice,
I think I know enough of hate
To say that for destruction ice
Is also great
And would suffice.

WILLIAM SHAKESPEARE
*When I Have Seen by Time's Fell Hand Defaced*

### LXIV

When I have seen by time's fell° hand defaced          *Destroying*
The rich-proud cost of outworn buried age;
When sometime° lofty towers I see down-razed,          *Formerly*
And brass eternal slave to mortal rage;
5  When I have seen the hungry ocean gain
Advantage on the kingdom of the shore,
And the firm soil win of the watery main,
Increasing store with loss, and loss with store;

When I have seen such interchange of state,
10  Or state itself confounded to decay,
Ruin hath taught me thus to ruminate,
That time will come and take my love away.
This thought is as a death, which cannot choose
But weep to have that which it fears to lose.


## Percy Bysshe Shelley
### *Ozymandias*

I met a traveler from an antique land
Who said: Two vast and trunkless legs of stone
Stand in the desert . . . Near them, on the sand,
Half sunk, a shattered visage lies, whose frown,
5  And wrinkled lip, and sneer of cold command,
Tell that its sculptor well those passions read
Which yet survive, stamped on these lifeless things,
The hand that mocked them, and the heart that fed:
And on the pedestal these words appear:
10  "My name is Ozymandias, king of kings:
Look on my works, ye Mighty, and despair!"
Nothing beside remains. Round the decay
Of that colossal wreck, boundless and bare
The lone and level sands stretch far away.

# Section VII

BEN JONSON

*To the Memory of My Beloved, the Author Mr. William Shakespeare*

And What He Hath Left Us

To draw no envy, Shakespeare, on thy name,
Am I thus ample to thy book and fame,
While I confess thy writings to be such
As neither man nor Muse can praise too much.
5 'Tis true, and all men's suffrage.° But these ways          *Consent*
Were not the paths I meant unto thy praise:
For silliest ignorance on these may light,
Which, when it sounds at best, but echoes right;
Or blind affection,° which doth ne'er advance          *Feeling*
10 The truth, but gropes, and urgeth all by chance;
Or crafty malice might pretend this praise,
And think to ruin where it seemed to raise.
These are as some infamous bawd or whore
Should praise a matron. What could hurt her more?
15 But thou art proof against them, and, indeed,
Above th' ill fortune of them, or the need.
I therefore will begin. Soul of the age!
The applause! delight! the wonder of our stage!
My Shakespeare, rise; I will not lodge thee by
20 Chaucer or Spenser, or bid Beaumont lie
A little further to make thee a room:°          *Chaucer, Spenser, and*
Thou art a monument without a tomb,          *Beaumont are all*
And art alive still while thy book doth live,          *buried in West-*
And we have wits to read and praise to give.          *minster Abbey*
25 That I not mix thee so, my brain excuses,
I mean with great, but disproportioned° Muses;          *Not com-*
For, if I thought my judgment were of years,          *parable*
I should commit thee surely with thy peers,
And tell how far thou didst our Lyly outshine,
30 Or sporting Kyd, or Marlowe's mighty line.
And though thou hadst small Latin and less Greek,
From thence to honor thee I would not seek
For names, but call forth thund'ring Aeschylus,
Euripides, and Sophocles to us,
35 Pacuvius, Accius, him of Cordova dead,°          *Pacuvius, Accius, and*
To life again, to hear thy buskin°          *Seneca ("him of Cordova")*
   tread          *were Roman tragedians.*
And shake a stage; or, when thy          *Buskin is the high-heeled*
   socks were on,          *boot worn by Greek tragic*

Leave thee alone for the comparison     *actors; the "sock" or*
Of all that insolent Greece or haughty Rome   *light shoe was worn*
40   Sent forth, or since did from their ashes come.    *by comic actors*
    Triumph, my Britain; thou hast one to show
    To whom all scenes° of Europe homage owe.      *Stages*
    He was not of an age, but for all time!
    And all the Muses still were in their prime
45   When like Apollo he came forth to warm
    Our ears, or like a Mercury to charm.
    Nature herself was proud of his designs,
    And joyed to wear the dressing of his lines,
    Which were so richly spun, and woven so fit,
50   As, since, she will vouchsafe no other wit:
    The merry Greek, tart Aristophanes,
    Neat Terence, witty Plautus° now not please,    *Aristophanes*
    But antiquated and deserted lie,     *(Greek) and Terence and*
    As they were not of Nature's family.     *Plautus (Roman) were*
55   Yet must I not give Nature all; thy Art,     *comic playwrights*
    My gentle Shakespeare, must enjoy a part.
    For though the poet's matter Nature be,
    His Art doth give the fashion; and that he
    Who casts to write a living line must sweat
60   (Such as thine are) and strike the second heat
    Upon the muses' anvil; turn the same,
    And himself with it, that he thinks to frame,
    Or for the laurel he may gain a scorn;
    For a good poet's made as well as born.
65   And such wert thou! Look how the father's face
    Lives in his issue, even so the race
    Of Shakespeare's mind and manners brightly shines
    In his well-turnéd and true-filéd lines,
    In each of which he seems to shake a lance,
70   As brandished at the eyes of ignorance.
    Sweet swan of Avon, what a sight it were
    To see thee in our waters yet appear,
    And make those flights upon the banks of Thames
    That so did take Eliza and our James!°    *Queen Elizabeth and*
75   But stay; I see thee in the hemisphere     *King James*
    Advanced and made a constellation there!
    Shine forth, thou star of poets, and with rage
    Or influence chide or cheer the drooping stage,
    Which, since thy flight from hence, hath mourned like
      night,
80   And despairs day, but for thy volume's light.

# Thomas Carew
## An Elegy upon the Death of the Dean of Paul's, Dr. John Donne

Can we not force from widowed poetry,
Now thou art dead, great Donne, one elegy
To crown thy hearse? Why yet did we not trust,
Though with unkneaded dough-baked prose, thy dust,
5   Such as the unscissored° lect'rer from the flower      *I.e., with*
Of fading rhetoric, short-lived as his hour,                   *uncut hair.*
Dry as the sand that measures it,° should lay       *I.e., the sand in*
Upon the ashes on the funeral day?                    *an hourglass*
Have we nor tune, nor voice? Didst thou dispense
10  Through all our language both the words and sense?
'Tis a sad truth. The pulpit may her plain
And sober Christian precepts still retain;
Doctrines it may, and wholesome uses, frame,
Grave homilies and lectures; but the flame
15  Of thy brave soul, that shot such heat and light
As burnt our earth and made our darkness bright,
Committed holy rapes upon our will,
Did through the eye the melting heart distil,
And the deep knowledge of dark truths so teach
20  As sense might judge what fancy could not reach,
Must be desired forever. So the fire
That fills with spirit and heat the Delphic choir,°     *The choir of*
Which, kindled first by thy Promethean° breath,    *poets. Delphi*
Glowed here a while, lies quenched now in thy death.   *was the*
25  The Muses' garden, with pedantic weeds        *site of an oracle of*
O'erspread, was purged by thee; the lazy seeds     *Apollo, the god*
Of servile imitation thrown away,                     *of poetry.*
And fresh invention planted; thou didst pay       *The fire which*
The debts of our penurious bankrupt age;    *Prometheus, a Titan*
30  Licentious thefts, that make poetic rage      *stole from Olympus*
A mimic fury, when our souls must be        *and gave to man; a*
Possessed, or with Anacreon's ecstasy,           *life-giving force.*
Or Pindar's,° not their own; the subtle cheat    *Anacreon and*
Of sly exchanges, and the juggling feat       *Pindar were Greek*
35  Of two-edged words, or whatsoever wrong        *poets*
By ours was done the Greek or Latin tongue,
Thou hast redeemed, and opened us a mine
Of rich and pregnant fancy, drawn a line
Of masculine expression, which had good

40  Old Orpheus° seen, or all the ancient brood          *In Greek*
Our superstitious fools admire, and hold      *mythology a Thracian*
Their lead more precious than thy burnished gold,          *poet and*
Thou hadst been their exchequer, and no more      *musician, son*
They in each other's dung had searched for ore.      *of one of the*
45  Thou shalt yield no precédence, but of time                *Muses*
And the blind fate of language, whose tuned chime
More charms the outward sense; yet thou mayest claim
From so great disadvantage greater fame,
Since to the awe of thy imperious wit
50  Our troublesome language bends, made only fit
With her tough thick-ribbed hoops, to gird about
Thy giant fancy, which had proved too stout
For their soft melting phrases. As in time
They had the start, so did they cull the prime
55  Buds of invention many a hundred year,
And left the rifled fields, besides the fear
To touch their harvest; yet from those bare lands
Of what is only thine, thy only hands
(And that their smallest work) have gleanéd more
60  Than all those times and tongues could reap before.
     But thou art gone, and thy strict laws will be
Too hard for libertines in poetry.
They will recall the goodly exiled train
Of gods and goddesses, which in thy just reign
65  Were banished nobler poems; now with these
The silenced tales i' th' *Metamorphoses*°      *Ovid's* Metamorphoses
Shall stuff their lines and swell the windy page,
Till verse, refined by thee in this last age,
Turn ballad-rhyme, or those old idols be
70  Adored again with new apostasy.
     O pardon me, that break with untuned verse
The reverend silence that attends thy hearse,
Whose solemn awful murmurs were to thee,
More than these faint lines, a loud elegy,
75  That did proclaim in a dumb eloquence
The death of all the arts, whose influence,
Grown feeble, in these panting numbers lies
Gasping short-winded accents, and so dies:
So doth the swiftly turning wheel not stand
80  In th' instant we withdraw the moving hand,
But some small time retain a faint weak course
By virtue of the first impulsive force;
And so whilst I cast on thy funeral pile

Thy crown of bays,° oh, let it crack awhile
85 And spit disdain, till the devouring flashes
Suck all the moisture up; then turn to ashes.
  I will not draw thee envy to engross
All thy perfections, or weep all the loss;
Those are too numerous for one elegy,
90 And this too great to be expressed by me.
Let others carve the rest; it shall suffice
I on thy grave this epitaph incise:

  *Here lies a king, that ruled as he thought fit*
  *The universal monarchy of wit;*
95 *Here lie two flamens,° and both those the best:*
  *Apollo's first, at last the true God's priest.*

*In classical times,*
*the reward of the*
*victor in a poetic*
*competition*

*Priests*

GEORGE GORDON, LORD BYRON
*On the Death of a Young Lady*
Cousin to the Author, and Very Dear to Him

  Hush'd are the winds, and still the evening gloom,
    Not e'en a zephyr° wanders through the grove,
  Whilst I return, to view my Margaret's tomb,
    And scatter flowers on the dust I love.

*The west*
*wind*

5 Within this narrow cell reclines her clay,
    That clay, where once such animation beam'd;
  The King of Terrors seized her as his prey,
    Not worth, nor beauty, have her life redeem'd.

  Oh! could that King of Terrors pity feel,
10    Or Heaven reverse the dread decrees of fate!
  Not here the mourner would his grief reveal,
    Not here the muse her virtues would relate.

  But wherefore weep? Her matchless spirit soars
    Beyond where splendid shines the orb of day;
15 And weeping angels lead her to those bowers
    Where endless pleasures virtue's deeds repay.

And shall presumptuous mortals Heaven arraign,
  And, madly, godlike Providence accuse?
Ah! no, far fly from me attempts so vain;—
20     I'll ne'er submission to my God refuse.

Yet is remembrance of those virtues dear,
  Yet fresh the memory of that beauteous face;
Still they call forth my warm affection's tear,
  Still in my heart retain their wonted place.


# EDGAR ALLAN POE
## *Annabel Lee*

It was many and many a year ago,
  In a kingdom by the sea,
That a maiden there lived whom you may know
  By the name of Annabel Lee;
5  And this maiden she lived with no other thought
  Than to love and be loved by me.

*She* was a child and *I* was a child,
  In this kingdom by the sea,
But we loved with a love that was more than love—
10     I and my Annabel Lee—
With a love that the wingéd seraphs of Heaven
  Coveted her and me.

And this was the reason that, long ago,
  In this kingdom by the sea,
15  A wind blew out of a cloud by night
  Chilling my Annabel Lee;
So that her highborn kinsmen came
  And bore her away from me,
To shut her up in a sepulchre
20     In this kingdom by the sea.

The angels, not half so happy in Heaven,
  Went envying her and me:
Yes! that was the reason (as all men know,
  In this kingdom by the sea)
25  That the wind came out of the cloud, chilling
  And killing my Annabel Lee.

But our love it was stronger by far than the love
        Of those who were older than we—
        Of many far wiser than we—
30   And neither the angels in Heaven above
        Nor the demons down under the sea,
Can ever dissever my soul from the soul
        Of the beautiful Annabel Lee:

For the moon never beams without bringing me dreams
35        Of the beautiful Annabel Lee;
And the stars never rise but I see the bright eyes
        Of the beautiful Annabel Lee;
And so, all the night-tide, I lie down by the side
Of my darling, my darling, my life and my bride,
40        In her sepulchre there by the sea—
        In her tomb by the side of the sea.

OSCAR WILDE
*Requiescat* *

    Tread lightly, she is near
        Under the snow,
    Speak gently, she can hear
        The daisies grow.

5   All her bright golden hair
        Tarnished with rust,
    She that was young and fair
        Fallen to dust.

    Lily-like, white as snow,
10      She hardly knew
    She was a woman, so
        Sweetly she grew.

    Coffin-board, heavy stone,
        Lie on her breast;
15   I vex my heart alone,
        She is at rest.

* A prayer for the repose of the dead.

Peace, peace; she cannot hear
　　Lyre or sonnet;
All my life's buried here.
20　　Heap earth upon it.


MATTHEW ARNOLD
*Requiescat*

Strew on her roses, roses,
　　And never a spray of yew!°　　　　　*Cone-bearing evergreen tree*
In quiet she reposes;
　　Ah, would that I did too!

5　Her mirth the world required;
　　She bathed it in smiles of glee
But her heart was tired, tired,
　　And now they let her be.

Her life was turning, turning,
10　　In mazes of heat and sound.
But for peace her soul was yearning,
　　And now peace laps her round.

Her cabined, ample spirit,
　　It fluttered and failed for breath.
15　Tonight it doth inherit
　　The vasty hall of death.

CHRISTINA ROSSETTI
*Song*

When I am dead, my dearest,
　　Sing no sad songs for me;
Plant thou no roses at my head,
　　Nor shady cypress tree:
5　Be the green grass above me
　　With showers and dewdrops wet:
And if thou wilt, remember,
　　And if thou wilt, forget.

I shall not see the shadows,
10    I shall not feel the rain;
I shall not hear the nightingale
    Sing on as if in pain:
And dreaming through the twilight
    That doth not rise nor set,
15  Haply I may remember,
    And haply may forget.


WILLIAM SHAKESPEARE
*No Longer Mourn for Me When I Am Dead*

### LXXI

No longer mourn for me when I am dead
Than you shall hear the surly sullen bell
Give warning to the world that I am fled
From this vile world, with vilest worms to dwell:
5   Nay, if you read this line, remember not
The hand that writ it; for I love you so,
That I in your sweet thoughts would be forgot,
If thinking on me then should make you woe.
Oh, if, I say, you look upon this verse
10  When I perhaps compounded am with clay,
Do not so much as my poor name rehearse,
But let your love even with my life decay;
Lest the wise world should look into your moan,
And mock you with me after I am gone.

KENNETH FEARING
*Dirge*

1-2-3 was the number he played but today the number came
    3-2-1;
Bought his Carbide at 30 and it went to 29; had the favorite at
    Bowie but the track was slow—

O executive type, would you like to drive a floating-power, knee-action, silk-upholstered six? Wed a Hollywood star? Shoot the course in 58? Draw to the ace, king, jack?

O fellow with a will who won't take no, watch out for three cigarettes on the same, single match; O democratic voter born in August under Mars, beware of liquidated rails—

5   Denouement to denouement, he took a personal pride in the certain, certain way he lived his own, private life,

But nevertheless, they shut off his gas; nevertheless, the bank foreclosed; nevertheless, the landlord called; nevertheless, the radio broke,

And twelve o'clock arrived just once too often,

Just the same he wore one gray tweed suit, bought one straw hat, drank one straight Scotch, walked one short step, took one long look, drew one deep breath,

Just one too many,

10   And wow he died as wow he lived,

Going whop to the office and blooie home to sleep and biff got married and bam had children and oof got fired,

Zowie did he live and zowie did he die,

With who the hell are you at the corner of his casket, and where the hell're we going on the right-hand silver knob, and who the hell cares walking second from the end with an American Beauty wreath from why the hell not,

Very much missed by the circulation staff of the New York Evening Post; deeply mourned by the B.M.T.°     *A New*
15   Wham, Mr. Roosevelt; pow, Sears Roebuck;    *York subway*
    awk, big dipper; bop, summer rain;         *line*

Bong, Mr., bong, Mr., bong, Mr., bong.


# E. E. CUMMINGS
## *nobody loses all the time*

i had an uncle named
Sol who was a born failure and
nearly everyone said he should have gone
into vaudeville perhaps because my Uncle Sol could

sing McCann He Was a Diver on Xmas Eve like Hell Itself which
may or may not account for the fact that my Uncle

Sol indulged in that possibly most inexcusable
of all to use a highfalootin phrase
luxuries that is or to
wit farming and be
it needlessly
added

my Uncle Sol's farm
failed because the chickens
ate the vegetables so
my Uncle Sol had a
chicken farm till the
skunks ate the chickens when

my Uncle Sol
had a skunk farm but
the skunks caught cold and
died and so
my Uncle Sol imitated the
skunks in a subtle manner

or by drowning himself in the watertank
but somebody who'd given my Uncle Sol a Victor
Victrola and records while he lived presented to
him upon the auspicious occasion of his decease a
scrumptious not to mention splendiferous funeral with
tall boys in black gloves and flowers and everything and

i remember we all cried like the Missouri
when my Uncle Sol's coffin lurched because
somebody pressed a button
(and down went
my Uncle
Sol

and started a worm farm)

ANONYMOUS
*The Voyage of Life*\*
*Old English Poem*

    Now is it most like   as if on ocean
    Across cold water   we sail in our keels,
    Over the wide sea   in our ocean-steeds,
    Faring on in our flood-wood.   Fearful the stream,
5    The tumult of waters,   whereon we toss
    In this feeble world.   Fierce are the surges
    On the ocean-lanes.   Hard was our life
    Before we made harbor   over the foaming seas.
    Then help was vouchsafed   when God's Spirit-Son
10    Guided us to the harbor of salvation   and granted us grace
    That we may understand   over the ship's side
    Where to moor our sea-steeds,   our ocean-stallions,
    Fast at anchor.   Let us fix our hope
    Upon that haven   which the Lord of heaven,
15    In holiness on high,   has opened by His Ascension.


ALFRED, LORD TENNYSON
*Crossing the Bar*

    Sunset and evening star,
        And one clear call for me!
    And may there be no moaning of the bar,
        When I put out to sea,

5    But such a tide as moving seems asleep,
        Too full for sound and foam,
    When that which drew from out the boundless deep
        Turns again home.

    Twilight and evening bell,
10        And after that the dark!
    And may there be no sadness of farewell,
        When I embark;

    For though from out our bourne° of Time and Place      *Domain*
        The flood may bear me far,

\* C. W. Kennedy, trans.

15  I hope to see my Pilot face to face
      When I have crossed the bar.

CHIEF JOHN BUCK
*Memorial Ode* *

### Chant

Now, listen, Ye who established the Great League,°          *The*
Now it has become old,                    *League of Five Iroquois*
Now there is nothing but wilderness.            *nations centered in*
Ye are in your graves who established it.        *western New York*
5   Ye have taken it with you and have placed it under you,
And there is nothing left but desert.
There you have taken your great minds.
That which you established, you have taken with you
Ye have placed under your heads what ye have established,
10  The Great League.

### Refrain

Woe, Woe! Hearken ye!
    We are diminished
Woe, woe!
    The land has become a thicket.
15  Woe, woe!
        The clear places are deserted
        They are in their graves who established it.
Woe, the Great League!
        Yet they declared it should endure.
20  The Great League, Woe!
        Their work has grown old
        We are become wretched. Woe!

---

* Translated by Mary Austin; delivered by Chief John Buck on the occasion
of Chief Red Jacket's reburial in Forest Lawn Cemetery in 1884.

## WALT WHITMAN
### Red Jacket (from Aloft)
[Impromptu on Buffalo City's monument to, and reburial
of the old Iroquois orator, October 9, 1884]

Upon this scene, this show,
Yielded to-day by fashion, learning, wealth,
(Nor in caprice alone—some grains of deepest meaning,)
Haply, aloft, (who knows?) from distant sky-clouds' blended
    shapes,
5  As some old tree, or rock or cliff, thrill'd with its soul,
Product of Nature's sun, stars, earth direct—a towering human
    form,
In hunting-shirt of film, arm'd with the rifle, a half-ironical
    smile curving its phantom lips,
Like one of Ossian's° ghosts looks down.     *Ossian was a*
    *legendary Gaelic hero*

## EDWIN ARLINGTON ROBINSON
### For a Dead Lady

No more with overflowing light
Shall fill the eyes that now are faded,
Nor shall another's fringe with night
Their woman-hidden world as they did.
5  No more shall quiver down the days
The flowing wonder of her ways,
Whereof no language may requite
The shifting and the many-shaded.

The grace, divine, definitive,
10  Clings only as a faint forestalling;
The laugh that love could not forgive
Is hushed, and answers to no calling;
The forehead and the little ears
Have gone where Saturn keeps the years;
15  The breast where roses could not live
Has done with rising and with falling.

The beauty, shattered by the laws
That have creation in their keeping,
No longer trembles at applause,
20   Or over children that are sleeping;
And we who delve in beauty's lore
Know all that we have known before
Of what inexorable cause
Makes Time so vicious in his reaping.


JOHN CROWE RANSOM
*Bells for John Whiteside's Daughter*

There was such speed in her little body,
And such lightness in her footfall,
It is no wonder her brown study
Astonishes us all.

5   Her wars were bruited in our high window.
We looked among orchard trees and beyond
Where she took arms against her shadow,
Or harried unto the pond

The lazy geese, like a snow cloud
10   Dripping their snow on the green grass,
Tricking and stopping, sleepy and proud,
Who cried in goose, Alas,

For the tireless heart within the little
Lady with rod that made them rise
15   From their noon apple-dreams and scuttle
Goose-fashion under the skies!

But now go the bells, and we are ready,
In one house we are sternly stopped
To say we are vexed at her brown study,
20   Lying so primly propped.

# Section VIII

## BEN JONSON
### This Is Mab, the Mistress-Fairy

This is Mab, the mistress-fairy,
That doth nightly rob the dairy,
And can hurt or help the churning
As she please, without discerning.

5   She that pinches country wenches
If they rub not clean their benches,
And with sharper nails remembers
When they rake not up their embers;
But if so they chance to feast her,
10  In a shoe she drops a tester.

This is she that empties cradles,
Takes out children, puts in ladles;
Trains forth midwives in their slumber
With a sieve the holes to number;
15  And then leads them from her boroughs
Home through ponds and water-furrows.

She can start our franklin's daughters
In their sleep with shrieks and laughters,
And on sweet Saint Anne's night
20  Feed them with a promised sight,
Some of husbands, some of lovers,
Which an empty dream discovers.


## WILLIAM SHAKESPEARE
### Mercutio's Queen Mab Speech
From Romeo and Juliet

She is the fairies' midwife, and she comes
In shape no bigger than an agate stone
On the forefinger of an alderman,
Drawn with a team of little atomies
5  Over men's noses as they lie asleep;
Her wagon spokes made of long spinners' legs,
The cover, of the wings of grasshoppers;
Her traces, of the smallest spider's web;

Her collars, of the moonshine's wat'ry beams;
10  Her whip, of cricket's bone; the lash, of film;
Her wagoner, a small grey-coated gnat,
Not half so big as a round little worm
Pricked from the lazy finger of a maid;
Her chariot is an empty hazelnut,
15  Made by the joiner squirrel or old grub,
Time out o' mind the fairies' coachmakers.
And in this state she gallops night by night
Through lovers' brains, and then they dream of love;
O'er courtiers' knees, that dream on curtsies straight;
20  O'er lawyers' fingers, who straight dream on fees;
O'er ladies' lips, who straight on kisses dream,
Which oft the angry Mab with blisters plagues,
Because their breaths with sweetmeats tainted are.
Sometimes she gallops o'er a courtier's nose,
25  And then dreams he of smelling out a suit;
And sometime comes she with a tithe-pig's tail
Tickling a parson's nose as 'a lies asleep,
Then dreams he of another benefice.
Sometimes she driveth o'er a soldier's neck,
30  And then dreams he of cutting foreign throats,
Of breaches, ambuscadoes, Spanish blades,
Of healths five fathom deep; and then anon
Drums in his ear, at which he starts and wakes,
And being thus frighted, swears a prayer or two
35  And sleeps again. This is that very Mab
That plats the manes of horses in the night
And bakes the elflocks in foul sluttish hairs,
Which once untangled much misfortune bodes.
This is the hag, when maids lie on their backs,
40  That presses them and learns them first to bear,
Making them women of good carriage.

WILLIAM BLAKE
*The Crystal Cabinet*

The Maiden caught me in the Wild,
Where I was dancing merrily;
She put me into her Cabinet
And Locked me up with a golden Key.

5  This Cabinet is formed of Gold
   And Pearl & Crystal shining bright,
   And within it opens into a World
   And a little lovely Moony Night.

   Another England there I saw,
10 Another London with its Tower,
   Another Thames & other Hills,
   And another pleasant Surrey Bower,

   Another Maiden like herself,
   Translucent, lovely, shining clear,
15 Threefold each in the other closed—
   O, what a pleasant trembling fear!

   O, what a smile! a threefold Smile
   Filled me, that like a flame I burned;
   I bent to Kiss the lovely Maid,
20 And found a Threefold Kiss returned.

   I strove to seize the inmost Form
   With ardor fierce & hands of flame,
   But burst the Crystal Cabinet,
   And like a Weeping Babe became—

25 A weeping Babe upon the wild,
   And Weeping Woman pale reclined
   And in the outward air again
   I filled with woes the passing Wind.

JOHN KEATS
*La Belle Dame sans Merci* *

   O what can ail thee, Knight at arms,
      Alone and palely loitering?
   The sedge° has withered from the Lake          *Tufts of grass growing*
      And no birds sing!                              *in wet ground*

5  O what can ail thee, Knight at arms,
      So haggard, and so woebegone?

* The Beautiful Lady Without Mercy.

The squirrel's granary is full
 And the harvest's done.


I see a lily on thy brow
10 With anguish moist and fever dew,
And on thy cheeks a fading rose
 Fast withereth too.


"I met a Lady in the Meads,°        *Meadows*
 Full beautiful, a faery's child,
15 Her hair was long, her foot was light
 And her eyes were wild.


"I made a Garland for her head,
 And bracelets too, and fragrant Zone;°    *Girdle*
She looked at me as she did love
20 And made sweet moan.


"I set her on my pacing steed
 And nothing else saw all day long,
For sidelong would she bend and sing
 A faery's song.


25 "She found me roots of relish sweet,
 And honey wild, and manna dew,
And sure in language strange she said
 'I love thee true.'


"She took me to her elfin grot
30 And there she wept and sighed full sore,
And there I shut her wild wild eyes
 With kisses four.


"And there she lull\u00e9d me asleep,
 And there I dreamed, Ah Woe betide!
35 The latest° dream I ever dreamt       *Last*
 On the cold hill side.


"I saw pale Kings, and Princes too,
 Pale warriors, death-pale were they all;
They cried, 'La belle dame sans merci
40 Thee hath in thrall!'

"I saw their starved lips in the gloam
    With horrid warning gapéd wide,
And I awoke, and found me here
    On the cold hill's side.

45 "And this is why I sojourn here,
    Alone and palely loitering;
Though the sedge is withered from the Lake
    And no birds sing."


WILLIAM BUTLER YEATS
*The Host of the Air*

O'Driscoll drove with a song,
The wild duck and the drake,
From the tall and the tufted reeds
Of the drear Hart Lake.

5 And he saw how the reeds grew dark
At the coming of night tide,
And dreamed of the long dim hair
Of Bridget his bride.

He heard while he sang and dreamed
10 A piper piping away,
And never was piping so sad,
And never was piping so gay.

And he saw young men and young girls
Who danced on a level place
15 And Bridget his bride among them,
With a sad and a gay face.

The dancers crowded about him,
And many a sweet thing said,
And a young man brought him red wine
20 And a young girl white bread.

But Bridget drew him by the sleeve,
Away from the merry bands,
To old men playing at cards
With a twinkling of ancient hands.

25 The bread and the wine had a doom,
   For these were the host of the air;
   He sat and played in a dream
   Of her long dim hair.

   He played with the merry old men
30 And thought not of evil chance,
   Until one bore Bridget his bride
   Away from the merry dance.

   He bore her away in his arms,
   The handsomest young man there,
35 And his neck and his breast and his arms
   Were drowned in her long dim hair.

   O'Driscoll scattered the cards
   And out of his dream awoke:
   Old men and young men and young girls
40 Were gone like a drifting smoke;

   But he heard high up in the air
   A piper piping away,
   And never was piping so sad,
   And never was piping so gay.

ALFRED, LORD TENNYSON
*The Lotos-Eaters* *

   "Courage!" he° said, and pointed toward the land,          *I.e.,*
   "This mounting wave will roll us shoreward soon."          *Odysseus*
   In the afternoon they came unto a land
   In which it seeméd always afternoon.
5  All round the coast the languid air did swoon,
   Breathing like one that hath a weary dream.
   Full-faced above the valley stood the moon;
   And, like a downward smoke, the slender stream
   Along the cliff to fall and pause and fall did seem.

* People who ate the fruit of the lotus, which produced forgetfulness. Odysseus'
visit to their island is described in Book IX, 82–97 of *The Odyssey*.

10 A land of streams! some, like a downward smoke,
   Slow-dropping veils of thinnest lawn,° did go;     *Sheer cotton*
   And some through wavering lights and shadows broke,     *fabric*
   Rolling a slumbrous sheet of foam below.
   They saw the gleaming river seaward flow
15 From the inner land; far off, three mountain-tops,
   Three silent pinnacles of aged snow,
   Stood sunset-flushed; and, dewed with showery drops,
   Up-clomb the shadowy pine above the woven copse.

   The charmèd sunset lingered low adown
20 In the red West; through mountain clefts the dale
   Was seen far inland, and the yellow down
   Bordered with palm, and many a winding vale
   And meadow, set with slender galingale;°     *A reed-like plant*
   A land where all things always seemed the same!
25 And around about the keel with faces pale,
   Dark faces pale against that rosy flame,
   The mild-eyed melancholy Lotos-eaters came.

   Branches they bore of that enchanted stem,
   Laden with flower and fruit, whereof they gave
30 To each, but whoso did receive of them
   And taste, to him the gushing of the wave
   Far far away did seem to mourn and rave
   On alien shores; and if his fellow spake,
   His voice was thin, as voices from the grave;
35 And deep-asleep he seemed, yet all awake,
   And music in his ears his beating heart did make.

   They sat them down upon the yellow sand,
   Between the sun and moon upon the shore;
   And sweet it was to dream of fatherland,
40 Of child, and wife, and slave; but evermore
   Most weary seemed the sea, weary the oar,
   Weary the wandering fields of barren foam.
   Then someone said, "We will return no more;"
   And all at once they sang, "Our island home
45 Is far beyond the wave; we will no longer roam."

### Choric Song

#### 1

There is sweet music here that softer falls
Than petals from blown roses on the grass,

Or night-dews on still waters between walls
Of shadowy granite, in a gleaming pass;
50 Music that gentlier on the spirit lies,
Than tired eyelids upon tired eyes;
Music that brings sweet sleep down from the blissful skies.
Here are cool mosses deep,
And through the moss the ivies creep,
55 And in the stream the long-leaved flowers weep,
And from the craggy ledge the poppy hangs in sleep.

### 2

Why are we weighed upon with heaviness,
And utterly consumed with sharp distress,
While all things else have rest from weariness?
60 All things have rest: why should we toil alone,
We only toil, who are the first of things,
And make perpetual moan,
Still from one sorrow to another thrown;
Nor ever fold our wings,
65 And cease from wanderings,
Nor steep our brows in slumber's holy balm;
Nor harken what the inner spirit sings,
"There is no joy but calm!"—
Why should we only toil, the roof and crown of things?

### 3

70 Lo! in the middle of the wood,
The folded leaf is wooed from out the bud
With winds upon the branch, and there
Grows green and broad, and takes no care,
Sun-steeped at noon, and in the moon
75 Nightly dew-fed; and turning yellow
Falls, and floats adown the air.
Lo! sweetened with the summer light,
The full-juiced apple, waxing over-mellow,
Drops in a silent autumn night.
80 All its allotted length of days
The flower ripens in its place,
Ripens and fades, and falls, and hath no toil,
Fast-rooted in the fruitful soil.

### 4

Hateful is the dark-blue sky,
85 Vaulted o'er the dark-blue sea.

Death is the end of life; ah, why
Should life all labor be?
Let us alone. Time driveth onward fast
And in a little while our lips are dumb.
90 Let us alone. What is it that will last?
All things are taken from us, and become
Portions and parcels of the dreadful past.
Let us alone. What pleasure can we have
To war with evil? Is there any peace
95 In ever climbing up the climbing wave?
All things have rest, and ripen toward the grave
In silence—ripen, fall, and cease:
Give us long rest or death, dark death, or dreamful ease.

## 5

How sweet it were, hearing the downward stream,
100 With half-shut eyes ever to seem
Falling asleep in a half-dream!
To dream and dream, like yonder amber light,
Which will not leave the myrrh-bush on the height;
To hear each other's whispered speech;
105 Eating the Lotos day by day,
To watch the crisping ripples on the beach,
And tender curving lines of creamy spray;
To lend our hearts and spirits wholly
To the influence of mild-minded melancholy;
110 To muse and brood and live again in memory,
With those old faces of our infancy
Heaped over with a mound of grass,
Two handfuls of white dust, shut in an urn of brass!

## 6

Dear is the memory of our wedded lives,
115 And dear the last embraces of our wives
And their warm tears; but all hath suffered change;
For surely now our household hearths are cold,
Our sons inherit us, our looks are strange,
And we should come like ghosts to trouble joy.
120 Or else the island princes° over-bold         *The princes who had*
Have eat our substance, and the minstrel sings         *remained in*
Before them of the ten years' war in Troy,         *Ithaca during the*
And our great deeds, as half-forgotten things.         *Trojan War.*
Is there confusion in the little isle?°         *I.e., Ithaca*

125 Let what is broken so remain.
　　The Gods are hard to reconcile;
　　'Tis hard to settle order once again.
　　There *is* confusion worse than death,
　　Trouble on trouble, pain on pain,
130 Long labor unto aged breath,
　　Sore tasks to hearts worn out by many wars
　　And eyes grown dim with gazing on the pilot-stars.

7

　　But, propt on beds of amaranth° and moly,　　　*A legendary*
　　How sweet—while warm airs lull us, blowing lowly—　　*flower*
135 With half-dropt eyelid still,　　　　　　*reputed not to fade*
　　Beneath a heaven dark and holy,
　　To watch the long bright river drawing slowly
　　His waters from the purple hill—
　　To hear the dewy echoes calling
140 From cave to cave through the thick-twined vine—
　　To watch the emerald-colored water falling
　　Through many a woven acanthus-wreath divine!
　　Only to hear and see the far-off sparkling brine,
　　Only to hear were sweet, stretched out beneath the pine.

8

145 The Lotos blooms below the barren peak,
　　The Lotos blows by every winding creek;
　　All day the wind breathes low with mellower tone;
　　Through every hollow cave and alley lone
　　Round and round the spicy downs the yellow Lotos-dust is
　　　　blown.
150 We have had enough of action, and of motion we,
　　Rolled to starboard, rolled to larboard, when the surge was
　　　　seething free,
　　Where the wallowing monster spouted his foam-fountains in the
　　　　sea.
　　Let us swear an oath, and keep it with an equal mind,
　　In the hollow Lotos-land to live and lie reclined
155 On the hills like Gods together, careless of mankind.
　　For they lie beside their nectar, and the bolts are hurled
　　Far below them in the valleys, and the clouds are lightly curled
　　Round their golden houses, girdled with the gleaming world;
　　Where they smile in secret, looking over wasted lands,
160 Blight and famine, plague and earthquake, roaring deeps and fiery
　　　　sands,

Clanging fights, and flaming towns, and sinking ships, and praying
    hands.
But they smile, they find a music centered in a doleful song
Steaming up, a lamentation and an ancient tale of wrong,
Like a tale of little meaning though the words are strong;
165 Chanted from an ill-used race of men that cleave the soil,
Sow the seed, and reap the harvest with enduring toil,
Storing yearly little dues of wheat, and wine and oil;
Till they perish and they suffer—some, 'tis whispered—down in
    hell
Suffer endless anguish, others in Elysian valleys dwell,
170 Resting weary limbs at last on beds of asphodel.°   *A plant of the*
Surely, surely, slumber is more sweet than toil, the shore     *lily*
Than labor in the deep mid-ocean, wind and wave     *family*
    and oar;
O, rest ye, brother mariners, we will not wander more.


SAMUEL TAYLOR COLERIDGE
*Kubla Khan* *
or a Vision in a Dream. A Fragment

    In Xanadu did Kubla Khan
    A stately pleasure dome decree:
    Where Alph, the sacred river, ran
    Through caverns measureless to man
5       Down to a sunless sea.
    So twice five miles of fertile ground
    With walls and towers were girdled round:
    And there were gardens bright with sinuous rills,
    Where blossomed many an incense-bearing tree;
10     And here were forests ancient as the hills,
    Enfolding sunny spots of greenery.

    But oh! that deep romantic chasm which slanted
    Down the green hill athwart a cedarn cover!
    A savage place! as holy and enchanted
15     As e'er beneath a waning moon was haunted
    By woman wailing for her demon lover!
    And from this chasm, with ceaseless turmoil seething,
    As if this earth in fast thick pants were breathing,
    A mighty fountain momently was forced:

* A Chinese ruler of the thirteenth century.

20  Amid whose swift half-intermittent burst
    Huge fragments vaulted like rebounding hail,
    Or chaffy grain beneath the thresher's flail:
    And 'mid these dancing rocks at once and ever
    It flung up momently the sacred river.
25  Five miles meandering with a mazy motion
    Through wood and dale the sacred river ran,
    Then reached the caverns measureless to man,
    And sank in tumult to a lifeless ocean:
    And 'mid this tumult Kubla heard from far
30  Ancestral voices prophesying war!

        The shadow of the dome of pleasure
        Floated midway on the waves;
        Where was heard the mingled measure
        From the fountain and the caves.
35  It was a miracle of rare device,
    A sunny pleasure dome with caves of ice!

        A damsel with a dulcimer°              *Harplike instrument*
        In a vision once I saw:
        It was an Abyssinian maid,
40      And on her dulcimer she played,
        Singing of Mount Abora.
        Could I revive within me
        Her symphony and song,
        To such a deep delight 'twould win me,
45  That with music loud and long,
    I would build that dome in air,
    That sunny dome! those caves of ice!
    And all who heard should see them there,
    And all should cry, Beware! Beware!
50  His flashing eyes, his floating hair!
    Weave a circle round him thrice,
    And close your eyes with holy dread,
    For he on honey-dew hath fed,
    And drunk the milk of Paradise.


EDGAR ALLAN POE
*The City in the Sea*

        Lo! Death has reared himself a throne
        In a strange city lying alone

Far down within the dim West,
Where the good and the bad and the worst and the best
Have gone to their eternal rest.
There shrines and palaces and towers
(Time-eaten towers that tremble not!)
Resemble nothing that is ours.
Around, by lifting winds forgot,
Resignedly beneath the sky
The melancholy waters lie.

No rays from the holy heaven come down
On the long night-time of that town;
But light from out the lurid sea
Streams up the turrets silently—
Gleams up the pinnacles far and free—
Up domes—up spires—up kingly halls—
Up fanes—up Babylon-like walls—
Up shadowy long-forgotten bowers
Of sculptured ivy and stone flowers—
Up many and many a marvelous shrine
Whose wreathéd friezes intertwine
The viol, the violet, and the vine.

Resignedly beneath the sky
The melancholy waters lie.
So blend the turrets and shadows there
That all seem pendulous in air,
While from a proud tower in the town
Death looks gigantically down.

There open fanes and gaping graves
Yawn level with the luminous waves;
But not the riches there that lie
In each idol's diamond eye—
Not the gaily-jeweled dead
Tempt the waters from their bed;
For no ripples curl, alas!
Along that wilderness of glass—
No swellings tell that winds may be
Upon some far-off happier sea—
No heavings hint that winds have been
On seas less hideously serene.

But lo, a stir is in the air!
The wave—there is a movement there!

As if the towers had thrust aside,
45  In slightly sinking, the dull tide—
As if their tops had feebly given
A void within the filmy Heaven.
The waves have now a redder glow—
The hours are breathing faint and low—
50  And when, amid no earthly moans,
Down, down that town shall settle hence,
Hell, rising from a thousand thrones,
Shall do it reverence.

# Section IX

# WILLIAM BUTLER YEATS
## Sailing to Byzantium *

### 1

That is no country for old men. The young
In one another's arms, birds in the trees
—Those dying generations—at their song,
The salmon-falls, the mackerel-crowded seas,
5   Fish, flesh, or fowl, commend all summer long
Whatever is begotten, born, and dies.
Caught in that sensual music all neglect
Monuments of unaging intellect.

### 2

An aged man is but a paltry thing,
10   A tattered coat upon a stick, unless
Soul clap its hands and sing, and louder sing
For every tatter in its mortal dress,
Nor is there singing school but studying
Monuments of its own magnificence;
15   And therefore I have sailed the seas and come
To the holy city of Byzantium.

### 3

O sages standing in God's holy fire
As in the gold mosaic of a wall,
Come from the holy fire, perne° in a gyre,°
20   And be the singing-masters of my soul.
Consume my heart away; sick with desire
And fastened to a dying animal
It knows not what it is; and gather me
Into the artifice of eternity.

*Perne: to move in
a spiral pattern;
Gyre: Circular or
spiral form*

### 4

25   Once out of nature I shall never take
My bodily form from any natural thing,
But such a form as Grecian goldsmiths make
Of hammered gold and gold enameling
To keep a drowsy Emperor awake;
30   Or set upon a golden bough to sing
To lords and ladies of Byzantium
Of what is past, or passing, or to come.

* Ancient capital of the Eastern Roman Empire.

## John Keats
*Ode on a Grecian Urn*

Thou still unravish'd bride of quietness,
  Thou foster-child of silence and slow time,
Sylvan° historian, who canst thus express        *Of the woods*
  A flowery tale more sweetly than our rhyme:
5 What leaf-fring'd legend haunts about thy shape
    Of deities or mortals, or of both,
      In Tempe° or the dales of Arcady?°    *Ancient provinces in*
What men or gods are these? What maidens loth?     *Greece,*
  What mad pursuit? What struggle to escape?    *symbols of*
10     What pipes and timbrels? What wild ecstasy?    *perfect*
                                               *pastoral land-*

Heard melodies are sweet, but those unheard       *scapes*
  Are sweeter; therefore, ye soft pipes, play on;
Not to the sensual ear, but, more endear'd,
  Pipe to the spirit ditties of no tone:
15 Fair youth, beneath the trees, thou canst not leave
    Thy song, nor ever can those trees be bare;
      Bold Lover, never, never canst thou kiss
Though winning near the goal—yet, do not grieve;
  She cannot fade, though thou hast not thy bliss,
20     For ever wilt thou love, and she be fair!

Ah, happy, happy boughs! that cannot shed
  Your leaves, nor ever bid the Spring adieu;
And, happy melodist, unwearied,
  For ever piping songs for ever new;
25 More happy love! more happy, happy love!
    For ever warm and still to be enjoy'd,
      For ever panting, and for ever young;
All breathing human passion far above,
  That leaves a heart high-sorrowful and cloy'd,
30     A burning forehead, and a parching tongue.

Who are these coming to the sacrifice?
  To what green altar, O mysterious priest,
Lead'st thou that heifer lowing at the skies,
  And all her silken flanks with garlands dressed?
35 What little town by river or sea shore,
    Or mountain-built with peaceful citadel,
      Is emptied of this folk, this pious morn?

And, little town, thy streets for evermore
    Will silent be; and not a soul to tell
40        Why thou are desolate, can e'er return.

O Attic° shape! Fair attitude! with brede°        *Classical, simple.*
    Of marble men and maidens over wrought,        *Woven pattern*
With forest branches and the trodden weed;
    Thou, silent form, dost tease us out of thought
45 As doth eternity: Cold Pastoral!
    When old age shall this generation waste,
        Thou shalt remain, in midst of other woe
Than ours, a friend to man, to whom thou say'st,
    "Beauty is truth, truth beauty,"—that is all
50        Ye know on earth, and all ye need to know.

DYLAN THOMAS
*In My Craft or Sullen Art*

In my craft or sullen art
Exercised in the still night
When only the moon rages
And the lovers lie abed
5 With all their griefs in their arms,
I labor by singing light
Not for ambition or bread
Or the strut and trade of charms
On the ivory stages
10 But for the common wages
Of their most secret heart.

Not for the proud man apart
From the raging moon I write
On these spindrift pages
15 Nor for the towering dead
With their nightingales and psalms
But for the lovers, their arms
Round the griefs of the ages,
Who pay no praise or wages
20 Nor heed my craft or art.

167

## ROBINSON JEFFERS
### Let Them Alone

If God has been good enough to give you a poet
Then listen to him. But for God's sake let him alone until he is
    dead; no prizes, no ceremony,
They kill the man. A poet is one who listens
To nature and his own heart; and if the noise of the world grows
    up around him, and if he is tough enough,
5   He can shake off his enemies but not his friends.
That is what withered Wordsworth and muffled Tennyson, and
    would have killed Keats; that is what makes
Hemingway play the fool and Faulkner forget his art.


## WILLIAM BUTLER YEATS
### To a Friend Whose Work Has Come to Nothing

Now all the truth is out,
Be secret and take defeat
From any brazen throat,
For how can you compete,
5   Being honor bred, with one
Who, were it proved he lies,
Were neither shamed in his own
Nor in his neighbors' eyes?
Bred to a harder thing
10  Than Triumph, turn away
And like a laughing string
Whereon mad fingers play
Amid a place of stone,
Be secret and exult,
15  Because of all things known
That is most difficult.

## WILLIAM SHAKESPEARE
### Not Marble, nor the Gilded Monuments

#### LV

Not marble, nor the gilded monuments
Of princes, shall outlive this powerful rhyme;

But you shall shine more bright in these conténts
Than unswept stone, besmeared with sluttish time.
5   When wasteful war shall statues overturn,
And broils root out the work of masonry,
Nor Mars his° sword nor war's quick fire shall burn        *I.e.,*
The living record of your memory.           *Mars' sword*
'Gainst death and all-oblivious enmity
10  Shall you pace forth; your praise shall still find room
Even in the eyes of all posterity
That wear this world out to the ending doom.
So, till the judgment that yourself arise,
You live in this, and dwell in lovers' eyes.

## ROBINSON JEFFERS
### *To the Stone-Cutters*

Stone-cutters fighting time with marble, you foredefeated
Challengers of oblivion
Eat cynical earnings, knowing rock splits, records fall down,
The square-limbed Roman letters
5   Scale in the thaws, wear in the rain. The poet as well
Builds his monument mockingly;
For man will be blotted out, the blithe earth die, the brave sun
Die blind and blacken to the heart:
Yet stones have stood for a thousand years, and pained thoughts
     found
10  The honey of peace in old poems.

## OWEN DODSON
### *Yardbird's Skull (for Charlie Parker)*

The bird is lost,
Dead, with all the music:
Whole sunsets heard the brain's music
Faded to last horizon notes.
5   I do not know why I hold
This skull, smaller than a walnut's,
Against my ear,

Expecting to hear
The smashed fear
10   Of childhood from . . . bone;
Expecting to see
Wind nosing red and purple,
Strange gold and magic
On bubbled windowpanes
15   Of childhood. Shall I hear?
I should hear: this skull
Has been with violets
Not Yorick, or the gravedigger,
Yapping his yelling story,
20   This skull has been in air,
Sensed his brother, the swallow,
(Its talent for snow and crumbs).
Flown to lost Atlantis islands,
Places of dreaming, swimming lemmings.
25   O I shall hear skull skull,
Hear your lame music,
Believe music rejects undertaking,
Limps back.
Remember tiny lasting, we get lonely:
30   Come sing, come sing, come sing sing
And sing.


Ted Joans
*Lester Young*

Sometimes he was cool like an eternal
        blue flame burning in the old Kansas
        City nunnery
Sometimes he was happy 'til he'd think
5        about his birth place and its blood
        stained clay hills and crow-filled trees
Most times he was blowin' on the wonderful
        tenor sax of his, preachin' in very cool
        tones, shouting only to remind you of
10       a certain point in his blue messages
He was our president as well as the minister
        of soul stirring Jazz, he knew what he
        blew, and he did what a prez should do,
        wail, wail, wail. There were many of

15    them to follow him and most of them were
      fair—but they never spoke so eloquently
      in so a far out funky air.
      Our prez done died, he know'd this would come
      but death has only booked him, alongside
20    Bird, Art Tatum, and other heavenly wailers.
      Angels of Jazz—they don't die—they live
      they live—in hipsters like you and I.

LOUIS SIMPSON
*Walt Whitman at Bear Mountain*

> *. . . life which does not give the preference to any other life, of any previous period,*
> *which therefore prefers its own existence . . .*
>                                                                —ORTEGA Y GASSET

      Neither on horseback nor seated,
      But like himself, squarely on two feet,
      The poet of death and lilacs
      Loafs by the footpath. Even the bronze looks alive
5     Where it is folded like cloth. And he seems friendly.

      "Where is the Mississippi panorama
      And the girl who played the piano?
      Where are you, Walt?
      The Open Road goes to the used-car lot.

10    "Where is the nation you promised?
      These houses built of wood sustain
      Colossal snows,
      And the light above the street is sick to death.

      "As for the people—see how they neglect you!
15    Only a poet pauses to read the inscription."

      "I am here," he answered.
      "It seems you have found me out.
      Yet, did I not warn you that it was Myself
      I advertised? Were my words not sufficiently plain?

20   "I gave no prescriptions,
And those who have taken my moods for prophecies
Mistake the matter."
Then, vastly amused—"Why do you reproach me?
I freely confess I am wholly disreputable.
25   Yet I am happy, because you have found me out."

A crocodile in wrinkled metal loafing . . .

Then all the realtors,
Pickpockets, salesmen, and the actors performing
Official scenarios,
30   Turned a deaf ear, for they had contracted
American dreams.

But the man who keeps a store on a lonely road,
And the housewife who knows she's dumb,
And the earth, are relieved.

35   All that grave weight of America
Cancelled! Like Greece and Rome.
The future in ruins!

The castles, the prisons, the cathedrals
Unbuilding, and roses
40   Blossoming from the stones that are not there . . .

The clouds are lifting from the high Sierras,
The Bay mists clearing.
And the angel in the gate, the flowering plum,
Dances like Italy, imagining red.


ALLEN GINSBERG
*A Supermarket in California*

What thoughts I have of you tonight, Walt Whitman, for I
walked down the sidestreets under the trees with a headache self-
conscious looking at the full moon.
In my hungry fatigue, and shopping for images, I went into
5   the neon fruit supermarket, dreaming of your enumerations!
What peaches and what penumbras°! Whole families

° Partly lighted area surrounding any area full of shadow.

shopping at night! Aisles full of husbands! Wives in the
avocados, babies in the tomatoes!—and you, Garcia Lorca,
what were you doing down by the watermelons?

10    I saw you, Walt Whitman, childless, lonely old grubber,
poking among the meats in the refrigerator and eyeing the grocery
boys.
    I heard you asking questions of each: Who killed the pork
chops? What price bananas? Are you my Angel?
15    I wandered in and out of the brilliant stacks of cans following
you, and followed in my imagination by the store detective.
    We strode down the open corridors together in our solitary
fancy tasting artichokes, possessing every frozen delicacy, and
never passing the cashier.

20    Where are we going, Walt Whitman? The doors close in an
hour. Which way does your beard point tonight?
    (I touch your book and dream of our odyssey in the supermarket
and feel absurd.)
    Will we walk all night through solitary streets? The trees add
25  shade to shade, lights out in the houses, we'll both be lonely.
    Will we stroll dreaming of the lost America of love past blue
automobiles in driveways, home to our silent cottage?
    Ah, dear father, graybeard, lonely old courage-teacher, what
America did you have when Charon° quit poling his ferry and
30  you got out on a smoking bank and stood watching the boat
disappear on the black waters of Lethe°?

WALT WHITMAN
*From* Song of Myself

52

The spotted hawk swoops by and accuses me, he complains of my
    gab and my loitering.

I too am not a bit tamed, I too am untranslatable,
I sound my barbaric yawp over the roofs of the world.

° Greek mythology; the boatman who ferried lost souls across the River
Styx.
° River of Forgetfulness flowing through Hades.

The last scud of day holds back for me,
5   It flings my likeness after the rest and true as any on the shadow'd
wilds,
It coaxes me to the vapor and the dusk.
I depart as air, I shake my white locks at the runaway sun,
I effuse my flesh in eddies, and drift it in lazy jags.

I bequeath myself to the dirt to grow from the grass I love,
10  If you want me again look for me under your boot-soles.

You will hardly know who I am or what I mean,
But I shall be good health to you nevertheless,
And filter and fiber your blood.

Failing to fetch me at first keep encouraged,
15  Missing me one place search another,
I stop somewhere waiting for you.


STEPHEN SPENDER
*I Think Continually of Those Who Were Truly Great*

I think continually of those who were truly great.
Who, from the womb, remembered the soul's history
Through corridors of light where the hours are suns,
Endless and singing. Whose lovely ambition
5   Was that their lips, still touched with fire,
Should tell of the spirit clothed from head to foot in song.
And who hoarded from the spring branches
The desires falling across their bodies like blossoms.

What is precious is never to forget
10  The delight of the blood drawn from ageless springs
Breaking through rocks in worlds before our earth;
Never to deny its pleasure in the simple morning light,
Nor its grave evening demand for love;
Never to allow gradually the traffic to smother
15  With noise and fog the flowering of the spirit.

Near the snow, near the sun, in the highest fields
See how those names are fêted by the waving grass,
And by the streamers of white cloud,
And whispers of wind in the listening sky;

20   The names of those who in their lives fought for life,
Who wore at their hearts the fire's centre.
Born of the sun they travelled a short while towards the sun,
And left the vivid air signed with their honour.

# Section X

## Anonymous
### *Sumer is i-cumen in*

Sumer is i-cumen in—
  Lhude sing, cuccu!
Groweth sed and bloweth med
  And springth the wude nu.
5      Sing, cuccu!

Awe bleteth after lomb,
  Lhouth after calve cu,
Bulluc sterteth, bucke verteth—
  Murie sing, cuccu!
10     Cuccu, cuccu.
  Wel singes thu, cuccu.
  Ne swik thu naver nu!

## Ezra Pound
### *Ancient Music*

Winter is icummen in,
Lhude sing Goddamm,
Raineth drop and staineth slop,
And how the wind doth ramm!
5           Sing: Goddamm.
Skiddeth bus and sloppeth us,
An ague hath my ham.
Freezeth river, turneth liver,
          Damn you, sing: Goddamm.
10  Goddamm, Goddamm, 'tis why I am, Goddamm,
         So 'gainst the winter's balm.
Sing goddamm, damm, sing Goddamm,
Sing goddamm, sing goddamm, DAMM.

## A. E. Housman
### *When I Was One-and-Twenty*

When I was one-and-twenty
  I heard a wise man say,

"Give crowns and pounds and guineas
    But not your heart away;
5  Give pearls away and rubies
    But keep your fancy free."
But I was one-and-twenty,
    No use to talk to me.

When I was one-and-twenty
10    I heard him say again,
"The heart out of the bosom
    Was never given in vain;
'Tis paid with sighs a plenty
    And sold for endless rue."
15  And I am two-and-twenty,
    And oh, 'tis true, 'tis true.


HUGH KINGSMILL [HUGH KINGSMILL LUNN]
*What, Still Alive at Twenty-two?*

What, still alive at twenty-two,
A clean upstanding chap like you?
Sure, if your throat 'tis hard to slit,
Slit your girl's, and swing for it.

5  Like enough, you won't be glad
When they come to hang you, lad:
But bacon's not the only thing
That's cured by hanging from a string.

So, when the spilt ink of the night
10  Spreads o'er the blotting-pad of light,
Lads whose job is still to do
Shall whet their knives, and think of you.

ALFRED, LORD TENNYSON
*The Charge of the Light Brigade*

Half a league, half a league,
    Half a league onward,

All in the valley of Death
  Rode the six hundred.
5  "Forward, the Light Brigade!
Charge for the guns!" he said.
Into the valley of Death
  Rode the six hundred.

"Forward, the Light Brigade!"
10  Was there a man dismayed?
Not though the soldier knew
  Someone had blundered.
Theirs not to make reply,
Theirs not to reason why,
15  Theirs but to do and die.
Into the valley of Death
  Rode the six hundred.

Cannon to right of them,
Cannon to left of them,
20  Cannon in front of them
  Volleyed and thundered;
Stormed at with shot and shell,
Boldly they rode and well,
Into the jaws of Death,
25  Into the mouth of Hell
  Rode the six hundred.

Flashed all their sabers bare,
Flashed as they turned in air
Sabring the gunners there,
30  Charging an army, while
  All the world wondered.
Plunged in the battery-smoke
Right through the line they broke;
Cossack and Russian
35  Reeled from the saber-stroke
  Shattered and sundered.
Then they rode back, but not,
  Not the six hundred.

Cannon to right of them,
40  Cannon to left of them,
Cannon behind them
  Volleyed and thundered;

Stormed at with shot and shell,
While horse and hero fell,
45 They that had fought so well
Came through the jaws of Death,
Back from the mouth of Hell,
All that was left of them,
   Left of six hundred.

50 When can their glory fade?
O the wild charge they made!
   All the world wondered.
Honor the charge they made!
Honor the Light Brigade,
55    Noble six hundred!


EZRA POUND
*The Charge of the Bread Brigade*

Half a loaf, half a loaf,
Half a loaf? Um-hum?
Down through the vale of gloom
Slouched the ten million,
5    Onward th' 'ungry blokes,
   Crackin' their smutty jokes!
We'll send 'em mouchin' 'ome,
Damn the ten million!

There goes the night brigade,
10 They got no steady trade,
Several old so'jers know
   Monty has blunder'd.
Theirs not to reason why,
Theirs but to buy the pie,
15 Slouching and mouching,
   Lousy ten million!

Plenty to right of 'em,
Plenty to left of 'em,
   Yes, wot is left of 'em,
20 Damn the ten million.
Stormed at by press and all,
How shall we dress 'em all?
   Glooming and mouching!

See 'em go slouching there,
25 With cowed and crouching air
    Dundering dullards!
How the whole nation shook
While Milord Beaverbrook
    Fed 'em with hogwash!

THOMAS GRAY
*Ode*
On the Death of a Favorite Cat, Drowned in a Tub of
Goldfishes

'Twas on a lofty vase's side,
Where China's gayest art had dyed
    The azure flowers that blow;°                    *Bloom*
Demurest of the tabby kind,
5  The pensive Selima, reclined,
    Gazed on the lake below.

Her conscious tail her joy declared;
The fair round face, the snowy beard,
    The velvet of her paws,
10 Her coat, that with the tortoise vies,
Her ears of jet, and emerald eyes,
    She saw; and purred applause.

Still had she gazed; but 'midst the tide
Two angel forms were seen to glide,
15     The genii° of the stream:                    *Guardian spirits*
Their scaly armor's Tyrian hue
Through richest purple to the view
    Betrayed a golden gleam.

The hapless nymph with wonder saw:
20 A whisker first and then a claw,
    With many an ardent wish,
She stretched in vain to reach the prize.
What female heart can gold despise?
    What cat's averse to fish?

Presumptuous maid! with looks intent
Again she stretched, again she bent,
    Nor knew the gulf between.
(Malignant Fate sat by and smiled)
The slippery verge her feet beguiled,
30      She tumbled headlong in.

Eight times emerging from the flood
She mewed to every watery god,
    Some speedy aid to send.
No dolphin came, no Nereid° stirred;    *Nereids are sea nymphs*
35  Nor cruel Tom, nor Susan heard;
    A favorite has no friend!

From hence, ye beauties, undeceived,
Know, one false step is ne'er retrieved,
    And be with caution bold.
40  Not all that tempts your wandering eyes
And heedless hearts, is lawful prize;
    Nor all that glisters, gold.

# ALEXANDER POPE
## *The Rape of the Lock*

*Nolueram, Belinda, tuos violare capillos;*
*sed juvat hoc precibus me tribuisse tuis.**
                                    —MARTIAL

### Canto I

    What dire offense from amorous causes springs,
What mighty contests rise from trivial things,
I sing—This verse to Caryll,† Muse! is due:
This, even Belinda may vouchsafe to view:
5   Slight is the subject, but not so the praise,
If she inspire, and he approve my lays.
    Say what strange motive, Goddess! could compel
A well-bred lord to assault a gentle belle?

* "I did not wish, Belinda, to violate your locks, but it pleases me to have paid this tribute to your prayers."
† John Caryll, a close friend of Pope, suggested that Pope write the poem to help end a quarrel between the families of Arabella Fermor and Lord Petre, which was caused by Lord Petre's actually cutting a lock of hair from the lady's head.

Oh, say what stranger cause, yet unexplored,
10 Could make a gentle belle reject a lord?
In tasks so bold can little men engage,
And in soft bosoms dwells such mighty rage?
　Sol through white curtains shot a timorous ray,
And oped those eyes that must eclipse the day.
15 Now lapdogs give themselves the rousing shake,
And sleepless lovers just at twelve awake:
Thrice rung the bell, the slipper knocked the ground,
And the pressed watch returned a silver sound.
Belinda still her downy pillow pressed,
20 Her guardian Sylph° prolonged the balmy rest:　　　*Air spirit*
'Twas he had summoned to her silent bed
The morning dream that hovered o'er her head.
A youth more glittering than a birthnight beau°　　*A courtier*
(That even in slumber caused her cheek to glow)　*dressed in*
25 Seemed to her ear his winning lips to lay,　　　*finery for a royal*
And thus in whispers said, or seemed to say:　　*birthday cele-*
　"Fairest of mortals, thou distinguished care　　*bration*
Of thousand bright inhabitants of air!
If e'er one vision touched thy infant thought,
30 Of all the nurse and all the priest have taught,
Of airy elves by moonlight shadows seen,
The silver token,° and the circled green,°　　*A coin left by a fairy*
Or virgins visited by angel powers,　　　　　*for a maiden whom he*
With golden crowns and wreaths of heavenly flowers,　*approves;*
35 Hear and believe! thy own importance know,　　*Grass-ringed*
Nor bound thy narrow views to things below.　*dancing circle of*
Some secret truths, from learned pride concealed,　*fairies*
To maids alone and children are revealed:
What though no credit doubting wits may give?
40 The fair and innocent shall still believe.
Know, then, unnumbered spirits round thee fly,
The light militia of the lower sky:
These, though unseen, are ever on the wing,
Hang o'er the box,° and hover round the Ring.°　*Theater box;*
45 Think what an equipage thou hast in air,　　　*Drive around Hyde*
And view with scorn two pages and a chair.°　　*Park;*
As now your own, our beings were of old,　　*Sedan chair*
And once enclosed in woman's beauteous mold;
Thence, by a soft transition, we repair
50 From earthly vehicles to these of air.
Think not, when woman's transient breath is fled,
That all her vanities at once are dead:

Succeeding vanities she still regards,
And though she plays no more, o'erlooks the cards.
55 Her joy in gilded chariots, when alive,
And love of ombre,° after death survive.                     *A popular*
For when the Fair in all their pride expire,               *card game.*
To their first elements° their souls retire:         *First elements: i.e.,*
The sprites of fiery termagants in flame               *fire, water, earth,*
60 Mount up, and take a Salamander's name.                      *and air*
Soft yielding minds to water glide away,
And sip, with Nymphs, their elemental tea.
The graver prude sinks downward to a Gnome,
In search of mischief still on earth to roam.
65 The light coquettes in Sylphs aloft repair,
And sport and flutter in the fields of air.
   "Know further yet; whoever fair and chaste
Rejects mankind, is by some Sylph embraced:
For spirits, freed from mortal laws, with ease
70 Assume what sexes and what shapes they please.
What guards the purity of melting maids,
In courtly balls, and midnight masquerades,
Safe from the treacherous friend, the daring spark,
The glance by day, the whisper in the dark,
75 When kind occasion prompts their warm desires,
When music softens, and when dancing fires?
'Tis but their Sylph, the wise Celestials know,
Though Honor is the word with men below.
   "Some nymphs there are, too conscious of their face,
80 For life predestined to the Gnomes' embrace.
These swell their prospects and exalt their pride,
When offers are disdained, and love denied:
Then gay ideas crowd the vacant brain,
While peers, and dukes, and all their sweeping train,
85 And garters, stars, and coronets° appear,            *Insignia of rank*
And in soft sounds, 'your Grace' salutes their ear.
'Tis these that early taint the female soul,
Instruct the eyes of young coquettes to roll,
Teach infant cheeks a bidden blush to know,
90 And little hearts to flutter at a beau.
   "Oft, when the world imagine women stray,
The Sylphs through mystic mazes guide their way,
Through all the giddy circle they pursue,
And old impertinence expel by new.
95 What tender maid but must a victim fall
To one man's treat, but for another's ball?

When Florio speaks what virgin could withstand,
If gentle Damon did not squeeze her hand?
With varying vanities, from every part,
100 They shift the moving toyshop of their heart;
Where wigs with wigs, with sword-knots
    sword-knots° strive,       *Ribbons tied to sword*
Beaux banish beaux, and coaches coaches drive.     *hilts*
This erring mortals levity may call;
Oh, blind to truth! the Sylphs contrive it all.
105   "Of these am I, who thy protection claim,
A watchful sprite, and Ariel is my name.
Late, as I ranged the crystal wilds of air,
In the clear mirror of thy ruling star
I saw, alas! some dread event impend,
110 Ere to the main this morning sun descend,
But Heaven reveals not what, or how, or where:
Warned by the Sylph, O pious maid, beware!
This to disclose is all thy guardian can:
Beware of all, but most beware of Man!"
115   He said; when Shock,° who thought she     *Belinda's lap dog*
    slept too long,
Leaped up, and waked his mistress with his tongue.
'Twas then, Belinda, if report say true,
Thy eyes first opened on a billet-doux;°       *A love letter*
Wounds, charms, and ardors were no sooner read,
120 But all the vision vanished from thy head.
    And now, unveiled, the toilet stands displayed,
Each silver vase in mystic order laid.
First, robed in white, the nymph intent adores,
With head uncovered, the cosmetic powers.
125 A heavenly image in the glass appears;
To that she bends, to that her eyes she rears.
The inferior priestess, at her altar's side,
Trembling begins the sacred rites of pride.
Unnumbered treasures ope at once, and here
130 The various offerings of the world appear;
From each she nicely culls with curious toil,
And decks the goddess with the glittering spoil.
This casket India's glowing gems unlocks,
And all Arabia breathes from yonder box.
135 The tortoise here and elephant unite,
Transformed to combs, the speckled and the white.
Here files of pins extend their shining rows,
Puffs, powders, patches, Bibles, billet-doux.

Now awful Beauty put on all its arms;
140 The fair each moment rises in her charms,
Repairs her smiles, awakens every grace,
And calls forth all the wonders of her face;
Sees by degrees a purer blush arise,
And keener lightnings quicken in her eyes.
145 The busy Sylphs surround their darling care,
These set the head, and those divide the hair,
Some fold the sleeve, whilst others plait the gown;
And Betty's praised for labors not her own.

## Canto II

Not with more glories, in the ethereal plain,
The sun first rises o'er the purpled main,
Than, issuing forth, the rival of his beams
Launched on the bosom of the silver Thames.
5 Fair nymphs and well-dressed youths around her shone,
But every eye was fixed on her alone.
On her white breast a sparkling cross she wore,
Which Jews might kiss, and infidels adore.
Her lively looks a sprightly mind disclose,
10 Quick as her eyes, and as unfixed as those:
Favors to none, to all she smiles extends;
Oft she rejects, but never once offends.
Bright as the sun, her eyes the gazers strike,
And, like the sun, they shine on all alike.
15 Yet graceful ease, and sweetness void of pride,
Might hide her faults, if belles had faults to hide:
If to her share some female errors fall,
Look on her face, and you'll forget 'em all.
This nymph, to the destruction of mankind,
20 Nourished two locks which graceful hung behind
In equal curls, and well conspired to deck
With shining ringlets the smooth ivory neck.
Love in these labyrinths his slaves detains,
And mighty hearts are held in slender chains.
25 With hairy springes° we the birds betray,          *Snares*
Slight lines of hair surprise the finny prey,
Fair tresses man's imperial race ensnare,
And beauty draws us with a single hair.
The adventurous Baron the bright locks admired,
30 He saw, he wished, and to the prize aspired.
Resolved to win, he meditates the way,
By force to ravish, or by fraud betray;

For when success a lover's toil attends,
Few ask if fraud or force attained his ends.
35    For this, ere Phoebus rose, he had implored
Propitious Heaven, and every power adored,
But chiefly Love—to Love an altar built,
Of twelve vast French romances, neatly gilt.
There lay three garters, half a pair of gloves,
40  And all the trophies of his former loves.
With tender billet-doux he lights the pyre,
And breathes three amorous sighs to raise the fire.
Then prostrate falls, and begs with ardent eyes
Soon to obtain, and long possess the prize:
45  The powers gave ear, and granted half his prayer,
The rest the winds dispersed in empty air.
    But now secure the painted vessel glides,
The sunbeams trembling on the floating tides,
While melting music steals upon the sky,
50  And softened sounds along the waters die.
Smooth flow the waves, the zephyrs gently play,
Belinda smiled, and all the world was gay.
All but the Sylph—with careful thoughts oppressed,
The impending woe sat heavy on his breast.
55  He summons straight his denizens° of air;       *Inhabitants.*
The lucid squadrons round the sails repair:°     *Assemble*
Soft o'er the shrouds aërial whispers breathe
That seemed but zephyrs to the train beneath.
Some to the sun their insect-wings unfold,
60  Waft on the breeze, or sink in clouds of gold.
Transparent forms too fine for mortal sight,
Their fluid bodies half dissolved in light,
Loose to the wind their airy garments flew,
Thin glittering textures of the filmy dew,°    *I.e., spider webs*
65  Dipped in the richest tincture of the skies,
Where light disports in ever-mingling dyes,
While every beam new transient colors flings,
Colors that change whene'er they wave their wings.
Amid the circle, on the gilded mast,
70  Superior by the head was Ariel placed;
His purple pinions opening to the sun,
He raised his azure wand, and thus begun:
    "Ye Sylphs and Sylphids, to your chief give ear!
Fays, Fairies, Genii, Elves, and Daemons, hear!
75  Ye know the spheres and various tasks assigned
By laws eternal to the aërial kind.

Some in the fields of purest ether play,
And bask and whiten in the blaze of day.
Some guide the course of wandering orbs on high,
80 Or roll the planets through the boundless sky.
Some less refined, beneath the moon's pale light
Pursue the stars that shoot athwart the night,
Or suck the mists in grosser air below,
Or dip their pinions in the painted bow,°     *Rainbow*
85 Or brew fierce tempests on the wintry main,
Or o'er the glebe° distill the kindly rain.     *Farmland*
Others on earth o'er human race preside,
Watch all their ways, and all their actions guide:
Of these the chief the care of nations own,
90 And guard with arms divine the British Throne.
 "Our humbler province is to tend the Fair,
Not a less pleasing, though less glorious care:
To save the powder from too rude a gale,
Nor let the imprisoned essences exhale;
95 To draw fresh colors from the vernal flowers;
To steal from rainbows e'er they drop in showers
A brighter wash; to curl their waving hairs,
Assist their blushes, and inspire their airs;
Nay oft, in dreams invention we bestow,
100 To change a flounce, or add a furbelow.
 "This day black omens threat the brightest fair,
That e'er deserved a watchful spirit's care;
Some dire disaster, or by force or slight,
But what, or where, the Fates have wrapped in night:
105 Whether the nymph shall break Diana's law,° *I.e., of chastity*
Or some frail china jar receive a flaw,
Or stain her honor or her new brocade,
Forget her prayers, or miss a masquerade,
Or lose her heart, or necklace, at a ball;
110 Or whether Heaven has doomed that Shock must fall.
Haste, then, ye spirits! to your charge repair:
The fluttering fan be Zephyretta's care;
The drops° to thee, Brillante, we consign;    *Earrings*
And, Momentilla, let the watch be thine;
115 Do thou, Crispissa, tend her favorite Lock;
Ariel himself shall be the guard of Shock.
 "To fifty chosen Sylphs, of special note,
We trust the important charge, the petticoat;
Oft have we known that sevenfold fence to fail,
120 Though stiff with hoops, and armed with ribs of whale.

Form a strong line about the silver bound,
And guard the wide circumference around.
  "Whatever spirit, careless of his charge,
His post neglects, or leaves the fair at large,
125 Shall feel sharp vengeance soon o'ertake his sins,
Be stopped in vials, or transfixed with pins,
Or plunged in lakes of bitter washes lie,
Or wedged whole ages in a bodkin's° eye;          *Large needle*
Gums and pomatums shall his flight restrain,
130 While clogged he beats his silken wings in vain,
Or alum styptics with contracting power
Shrink his thin essence like a riveled° flower:       *Shriveled*
Or, as Ixion fixed, the wretch shall feel
The giddy motion of the whirling mill,°       *In Greek mythology,*
135 In fumes of burning chocolate shall glow,       *Ixion was bound to*
And tremble at the sea that froths below!"       *a turning wheel*
  He spoke; the spirits from the sails descend;
Some, orb in orb, around the nymph extend;
Some thread the mazy ringlets of her hair;
140 Some hang upon the pendants of her ear:
With beating hearts the dire event they wait,
Anxious, and trembling for the birth of Fate.

### Canto III

  Close by those meads, forever crowned with flowers,
Where Thames with pride surveys his rising towers,
There stands a structure of majestic frame,°       *Hampton Court*
Which from the neighboring Hampton takes its name.
5 Here Britain's statesmen oft the fall foredoom
Of foreign tyrants and of nymphs at home;
Here thou, great Anna! whom three realms obey,
Don't sometimes counsel take—and sometimes tea.
  Hither the heroes and the nymphs resort,
10 To taste awhile the pleasures of a court;
In various talk the instructive hours they passed,
Who gave the ball, or paid the visit last;
One speaks the glory of the British Queen,
And one describes a charming Indian screen;
15 A third interprets motions, looks, and eyes;
At every word a reputation dies.
Snuff, or the fan, supply each pause of chat,
With singing, laughing, ogling, and all that.
  Meanwhile, declining from the noon of day,
20 The sun obliquely shoots his burning ray;

The hungry judges soon the sentence sign,
And wretches hang that jurymen may dine;
The merchant from the Exchange returns in peace,
And the long labors of the toilet cease.
25  Belinda now, whom thirst of fame invites,
Turns to encounter two adventurous knights,
At ombre singly to decide their doom,
And swells her breast with conquests yet to come.
Straight the three bands prepare in arms to join,
30  Each band the number of the sacred nine.
Soon as she spreads her hand, the aërial guard
Descend, and sit on each important card:
First Ariel perched upon a Matadore,
Then each according to the rank they bore;
35  For Sylphs, yet mindful of their ancient race,
Are, as when women, wondrous fond of place.
   Behold, four Kings in majesty revered,
With hoary whiskers and a forky beard;
And four fair Queens whose hands sustain a flower,
40  The expressive emblem of their softer power;
Four Knaves in garbs succinct, a trusty band,
Caps on their heads, and halberts in their hand;
And parti-colored troops, a shining train,
Draw forth to combat on the velvet plain.
45     The skillful nymph reviews her force with care;
"Let Spades be trumps!" she said, and trumps they were.
   Now move to war her sable Matadores,
In show like leaders of the swarthy Moors.
Spadillio first, unconquerable lord!
50  Led off two captive trumps, and swept the board.
As many more Manillio forced to yield,
And marched a victor from the verdant field.
Him Basto followed, but his fate more hard
Gained but one trump and one plebeian card.
55  With his broad saber next, a chief in years,
The hoary Majesty of Spades appears,
Puts forth one manly leg, to sight revealed,
The rest his many-colored robe concealed.
The rebel Knave, who dares his prince engage,
60  Proves the just victim of his royal rage.
Even mighty Pam,° that kings and queens o'erthrew        *I.e., jack*
And mowed down armies in the fights of loo,              *of clubs*
Sad chance of war! now distitute of aid,
Falls undistinguished by the victor Spade.

65  Thus far both armies to Belinda yield;
    Now to the Baron fate inclines the field.
    His warlike amazon her host invades,
    The imperial consort of the crown of Spades.
    The Club's black tyrant first her victim died,
70  Spite of his haughty mien and barbarous pride.
    What boots the regal circle on his head,
    His giant limbs, in state unwieldy spread?
    That long behind he trails his pompous robe,
    And of all monarchs only grasps the globe?
75  The Baron now his Diamonds pours apace;
    The embroidered King who shows but half his face,
    And his refulgent Queen, with powers combined
    Of broken troops an easy conquest find.
    Clubs, Diamonds, Hearts, in wild disorder seen,
80  With throngs promiscuous strew the level green.
    Thus when dispersed a routed army runs,
    Of Asia's troops, and Afric's sable sons,
    With like confusion different nations fly,
    Of various habit,° and of various dye,°          *Dress; Color*
85  The pierced battalions disunited fall
    In heaps on heaps; one fate o'erwhelms them all.
        The Knave of Diamonds tries his wily arts,
    And wins (oh, shameful chance!) the Queen of Hearts.
    At this, the blood the virgin's cheek forsook,
90  A livid paleness spreads o'er all her look;
    She sees, and trembles at the approaching ill,
    Just in the jaws of ruin, and Codille,
    And now (as oft in some distempered state)
    On one nice trick depends the general fate.
95  An Ace of Hearts steps forth: the King unseen
    Lurked in her hand, and mourned his captive Queen.
    He springs to vengeance with an eager pace,
    And falls like thunder on the prostrate Ace.
    The nymph exulting fills with shouts the sky,
100 The walls, the woods, and long canals° reply.          *Passages*
        O thoughtless mortals! ever blind to fate,          *between trees*
    Too soon dejected, and too soon elate:
    Sudden these honors shall be snatched away,
    And cursed forever this victorious day.
105     For lo! the board with cups and spoons is crowned,
    The berries crackle, and the mill turns round;°          *I.e., grinding*
    On shining altars of Japan° they raise          *coffee beans.*
    The silver lamp; the fiery spirits blaze:          *Lacquered tables*

From silver spouts the grateful liquors glide,
110 While China's earth° receives the smoking tide.　　*Ceramic cups*
At once they gratify their scent and taste,
And frequent cups prolong the rich repast.
Straight hover round the fair her airy band;
Some, as she sipped, the fuming liquor fanned,
115 Some o'er her lap their careful plumes displayed,
Trembling, and conscious of the rich brocade.
Coffee (which makes the politician wise,
And see through all things with his half-shut eyes)
Sent up in vapors to the Baron's brain
120 New stratagems, the radiant Lock to gain.
Ah, cease, rash youth! desist ere 'tis too late,
Fear the just Gods, and think of Scylla's fate!°　　*Scylla was*
Changed to a bird, and sent to flit in air,　　*changed to a bird as*
She dearly pays for Nisus' injured hair!　　*punishment for pulling*
125 　　But when to mischief mortals bend their will,　　*the golden*
How soon they find fit instruments of ill!　　*lock, on which her*
Just then, Clarissa drew with tempting grace　　*father's life*
A two-edged weapon from her shining case:　　*depended, from*
So ladies in romance assist their knight,　　*his head*
130 Present the spear, and arm him for the fight.
He takes the gift with reverence, and extends
The little engine on his fingers' ends;
This just behind Belinda's neck he spread,
As o'er the fragrant steams she bends her head.
135 Swift to the Lock a thousand sprites° repair,　　*Spirits*
A thousand wings, by turns, blow back the hair,
And thrice they twitched the diamond in her ear,
Thrice she looked back, and thrice the foe drew near.
Just in that instant, anxious Ariel sought
140 The close recesses of the virgin's thought;
As on the nosegay in her breast reclined,
He watched the ideas rising in her mind,
Sudden he viewed, in spite of all her art,
An earthly lover lurking at her heart.
145 Amazed, confused, he found his power expired,
Resigned to fate, and with a sigh retired.
　　The Peer now spreads the glittering forfex° wide,　　*Scissors*
To enclose the Lock; now joins it, to divide.
Even then, before the fatal engine closed,
150 A wretched Sylph too fondly interposed;
Fate urged the shears, and cut the Sylph in twain
(But airy substance soon unites again):

The meeting points the sacred hair dissever
From the fair head, forever, and forever!
155     Then flashed the living lightning from her eyes,
And screams of horror rend the affrighted skies.
Not louder shrieks to pitying heaven are cast,
When husbands, or when lapdogs breathe their last;
Or when rich china vessels fallen from high,
160 In glittering dust and painted fragments lie!
"Let wreaths of triumph now my temples twine,"
The victor cried, "the glorious prize is mine!
While fish in streams, or birds delight in air,
Or in a coach and six the British Fair,
165 As long as *Atalantis*° shall be read,      *A contemporary book*
Or the small pillow grace a lady's bed,      *recounting actual*
While visits shall be paid on solemn days,      *scandals*
When numerous wax-lights in bright order blaze,
While nymphs take treats, or assignations give,
170 So long my honor, name, and praise shall live!
What Time would spare, from Steel receives its date,°     *Termination*
And monuments, like men, submit to fate!
Steel could the labor of the Gods destroy,
And strike to dust the imperial towers of Troy;
175 Steel could the works of mortal pride confound,
And hew triumphal arches to the ground.
What wonder then, fair nymph! thy hairs should feel,
The conquering force of unresisted Steel?"

## Canto IV

    But anxious cares the pensive nymph oppressed,
And secret passions labored in her breast.
Not youthful kings in battle seized alive,
Not scornful virgins who their charms survive,
5 Not ardent lovers robbed of all their bliss,
Not ancient ladies when refused a kiss,
Not tyrants fierce that unrepenting die,
Not Cynthia° when her manteau's pinned awry,      *Diana,*
E'er felt such rage, resentment, and despair,      *goddess of chastity*
10 As thou, sad virgin! for thy ravished hair.
    For, that sad moment, when the Sylphs withdrew
And Ariel weeping from Belinda flew,
Umbriel, a dusky, melancholy sprite
As ever sullied the fair face of light,
15 Down to the central earth, his proper scene,
Repaired to search the gloomy Cave of Spleen.

Swift on his sooty pinions flits the Gnome,
And in a vapor reached the dismal dome.
No cheerful breeze this sullen region knows,
20 The dreaded east is all the wind that blows.
Here in a grotto, sheltered close from air,
And screened in shades from day's detested glare,
She sighs forever on her pensive bed,
Pain at her side, and Megrim° at her head.                    *Migraine*
25   Two handmaids wait the throne: alike in place,
But differing far in figure and in face.
Here stood Ill-Nature like an ancient maid,
Her wrinkled form in black and white arrayed;
With store of prayers for mornings, nights, and noons,
30 Her hand is filled; her bosom with lampoons.°              *Slanders*
There Affectation, with a sickly mien,
Shows in her cheek the roses of eighteen,
Practiced to lisp, and hang the head aside,
Faints into airs, and languishes with pride,
35 On the rich quilt sinks with becoming woe,
Wrapped in a gown, for sickness and for show.
The fair ones feel such maladies as these,
When each new nightdress gives a new disease.
A constant vapor o'er the palace flies,
40 Strange phantoms rising as the mists arise;
Dreadful as hermit's dreams in haunted shades,
Or bright as visions of expiring maids.
Now glaring fiends, and snakes on rolling spires,°            *Coils*
Pale specters, gaping tombs, and purple fires;
45 Now lakes of liquid gold, Elysian scenes,
And crystal domes, and angels in machines.
Unnumbered throngs on every side are seen
Of bodies changed to various forms by Spleen.
Here living teapots stand, one arm held out,
50 One bent; the handle this, and that the spout:
A pipkin° there, like Homer's tripod,° walks;          *Earthen pot;*
Here sighs a jar, and there a goose pie talks;          *Three-legged*
Men prove with child, as powerful fancy works,                *stool*
And maids, turned bottles, call aloud for corks.
55   Safe passed the Gnome through this fantastic band,
A branch of healing spleenwort° in his hand.        *A kind of fern,*
Then thus addressed the Power: "Hail, wayward          *believed*
     Queen!                                          *capable of purging*
Who rule the sex to fifty from fifteen:                     *spleen*
Parent of vapors and of female wit,
60 Who give the hysteric or poetic fit,

196

On various tempers act by various ways,
Make some take physic, others scribble plays;
Who cause the proud their visits to delay,
And send the godly in a pet to pray.
65  A nymph there is that all thy power disdains,
And thousands more in equal mirth maintains.
But oh! if e'er thy Gnome could spoil a grace,
Or raise a pimple on a beauteous face,
Like citron-waters° matrons' cheeks inflame,    *A kind of brandy*
70  Or change complexions at a losing game;   *made from orange peels.*
If e'er with airy horns I planted heads,°      *I.e., made men*
Or rumpled petticoats, or tumbled beds,    *imagine they had*
Or caused suspicion when no soul was rude,   *been cuckolded*
Or discomposed the headdress of a prude,
75  Or e'er to costive lapdog gave disease,
Which not the tears of brightest eyes could ease,
Hear me, and touch Belinda with chagrin.
That single act gives half the world the spleen."
    The Goddess with a discontented air
80  Seems to reject him though she grants his prayer.
A wondrous bag with both her hands she binds,
Like that where once Ulysses held the winds;°   *Aeolus, the god*
There she collects the force of female lungs,   *of winds, gave*
Sighs, sobs, and passions, and the war of     *Ulysses a bag*
      tongues.                           *containing all*
85  A vial next she fills with fainting fears,    *adverse winds*
Soft sorrows, melting griefs, and flowing tears.
The Gnome rejoicing bears her gifts away,
Spreads his black wings, and slowly mounts to day.
    Sunk in Thalestris'° arms the nymph he found,   *Thalestris*
90  Her eyes dejected and her hair unbound.    *was queen of the*
Full o'er their heads the swelling bag he rent,   *Amazons*
And all the Furies issued at the vent.
Belinda burns with more than mortal ire,
And fierce Thalestris fans the rising fire.
95  "O wretched maid!" she spreads her hands, and cried
(While Hampton's echoes, "Wretched maid!" replied),
"Was it for this you took such constant care
The bodkin,° comb, and essence to prepare?    *Hairpin*
For this your locks in paper durance bound,
100  For this with torturing irons wreathed around?
For this with fillets° strained your tender head,    *Bands.*
And bravely bore the double loads of lead?°   *Lead strips were*
Gods! shall the ravisher display your hair,   *used to hold curl*
While the fops envy, and the ladies stare!   *papers in place*

105 Honor forbid! at whose unrivaled shrine
Ease, pleasure, virtue, all, our sex resign.
Methinks already I your tears survey,
Already hear the horrid things they say,
Already see you a degraded toast,
110 And all your honor in a whisper lost!
How shall I, then, your helpless fame defend?
'Twill then be infamy to seem your friend!
And shall this prize, the inestimable prize,
Exposed through crystal to the gazing eyes,
115 And heightened by the diamond's circling rays,
On that rapacious hand forever blaze?
Sooner shall grass in Hyde Park Circus grow,
And wits take lodgings in the sound of Bow;°          *I.e., the bells*
Sooner let earth, air, sea, to chaos fall,          *of Bow Church in the*
120 Men, monkeys, lapdogs, parrots, perish all!"          *lower-class,*
    She said; then raging to Sir Plume repairs,          *commercial section*
And bids her beau demand the precious hairs          *of London*
(Sir Plume of amber snuffbox justly vain,
And the nice conduct of a clouded cane).
125 With earnest eyes, and round unthinking face,
He first the snuffbox opened, then the case,
And thus broke out—"My Lord, why, what the devil!
Zounds! damn the lock! 'fore Gad, you must be civil!
Plague on't! 'tis past a jest—nay prithee, pox!
130 Give her the hair"—he spoke, and rapped his box.
    "It grieves me much," replied the Peer again,
"Who speaks so well should ever speak in vain.
But by this Lock, this sacred Lock I swear
(Which never more shall join its parted hair;
135 Which never more its honors shall renew,
Clipped from the lovely head where late it grew),
That while my nostrils draw the vital air,
This hand, which won it, shall forever wear."
He spoke, and speaking, in proud triumph spread
140 The long-contended honors of her head.
    But Umbriel, hateful Gnome, forbears not so;
He breaks the vial whence the sorrows flow.
Then see! the nymph in beauteous grief appears,
Her eyes half languishing, half drowned in tears;
145 On her heaved bosom hung her drooping head,
Which with a sigh she raised, and thus she said:
    "Forever cursed be this detested day,
Which snatched my best, my favorite curl away!

Happy! ah, ten times happy had I been,
150 If Hampton Court these eyes had never seen!
Yet am not I the first mistaken maid,
By love of courts to numerous ills betrayed.
Oh, had I rather unadmired remained
In some lone isle, or distant northern land;
155 Where the gilt chariot never marks the way,
Where none learn ombre, none e'er taste bohea!°     *A kind*
There kept my charms concealed from mortal eye,     *of tea*
Like roses that in deserts bloom and die.
What moved my mind with youthful lords to roam?
160 Oh, had I stayed, and said my prayers at home!
'Twas this the morning omens seemed to tell,
Thrice from my trembling hand the patch box° fell;     *A box*
The tottering china shook without a wind,     *for ornamental*
Nay, Poll sat mute, and Shock was most unkind!     *patches to*
165 A Sylph too warned me of the threats of fate,     *accent the*
In mystic visions, now believed too late!     *face*
See the poor remnants of these slighted hairs!
My hands shall rend what e'en thy rapine spares.
These in two sable ringlets taught to break,
170 Once gave new beauties to the snowy neck;
The sister lock now sits uncouth, alone,
And in its fellow's fate foresees its own;
Uncurled it hangs, the fatal shears demands,
And tempts once more thy sacrilegious hands.
175 Oh, hadst thou, cruel! been content to seize
Hairs less in sight, or any hairs but these!"

### Canto V

She said: the pitying audience melt in tears.
But Fate and Jove had stopped the Baron's ears.
In vain Thalestris with reproach assails,
For who can move when fair Belinda fails?
5 Not half so fixed the Trojan could remain,
While Anna begged and Dido raged in vain.°     *Aeneas, when he*
Then grave Clarissa graceful waved her fan;     *decided to leave*
Silence ensued, and thus the nymph began:     *Carthage, was*
   "Say why are beauties praised and honored     *unmoved by*
       most,     *the pleadings of*
10 The wise man's passion, and the vain man's toast?     *Dido and*
Why decked with all that land and sea afford,     *Anna to*
Why angels called, and angel-like adored?     *remain*

Why round our coaches crowd the white-gloved beaux,
Why bows the side box from its inmost rows?
How vain are all these glories, all our pains,
Unless good sense preserve what beauty gains;
That men may say when we the front box grace,
'Behold the first in virtue as in face!'
Oh! if to dance all night, and dress all day,
Charmed the smallpox, or chased old age away,
Who would not scorn what housewife's cares produce,
Or who would learn one earthly thing of use?
To patch, nay ogle, might become a saint,
Nor could it sure be such a sin to paint.
But since, alas! frail beauty must decay,
Curled or uncurled, since locks will turn to gray;
Since painted, or not painted, all shall fade,
And she who scorns a man must die a maid;
What then remains but well our power to use,
And keep good humor still whate'er we lose?
And trust me, dear, good humor can prevail
When airs, and flights, and screams, and scolding fail.
Beauties in vain their pretty eyes may roll;
Charms strike the sight, but merit wins the soul."

So spoke the dame, but no applause ensued;
Belinda frowned, Thalestris called her prude.
"To arms, to arms!" the fierce virago cries,
And swift as lightning to the combat flies.
All side in parties, and begin the attack;
Fans clap, silks rustle, and tough whalebones crack;
Heroes' and heroines' shouts confusedly rise,
And bass and treble voices strike the skies.
No common weapons in their hands are found,
Like Gods they fight, nor dread a mortal wound.

So when bold Homer makes the Gods engage,
And heavenly breasts with human passions rage;
'Gainst Pallas, Mars; Latona, Hermes arms,° *In Iliad XX, the*
And all Olympus rings with loud alarms: *battle between the*
Jove's thunder roars, heaven trembles all around, *gods and*
Blue Neptune storms, the bellowing deeps resound: *goddesses*
Earth shakes her nodding towers, the ground gives way,
And the pale ghosts start at the flash of day!

Triumphant Umbriel on a sconce's height
Clapped his glad wings, and sat to view the fight:
Propped on the bodkin spears, the sprites survey
The growing combat, or assist the fray.

While through the press enraged Thalestris flies,
And scatters death around from both her eyes,
A beau and witling perished in the throng,
60 One died in metaphor, and one in song.
"O cruel nymph! a living death I bear,"
Cried Dapperwit, and sunk beside his chair.
A mournful glance Sir Fopling upwards cast,
"Those eyes are made so killing"—was his last.
65 Thus on Maeander's flowery margin lies
The expiring swan, and as he sings he dies.
When bold Sir Plume had drawn Clarissa down,
Chloe stepped in, and killed him with a frown;
She smiled to see the doughty hero slain,
70 But, at her smile, the beau revived again.
Now Jove suspends his golden scales in air,
Weighs the men's wits against the lady's hair;
The doubtful beam long nods from side to side;
At length the wits mount up, the hairs subside.
75 See, fierce Belinda on the Baron flies,
With more than usual lightning in her eyes;
Nor feared the chief the unequal fight to try,
Who sought no more than on his foe to die.
But this bold lord with manly strength endued,
80 She with one finger and a thumb subdued:
Just where the breath of life his nostrils drew,
A charge of snuff the wily virgin threw;
The Gnomes direct, to every atom just,
The pungent grains of titillating dust.
85 Sudden, with starting tears each eye o'erflows,
And the high dome re-echoes to his nose.
"Now meet thy fate," incensed Belinda cried,
And drew a deadly bodkin from her side.
(The same, his ancient personage to deck,
90 Her great-great-grandsire wore about his neck,
In three seal rings; which after, melted down,
Formed a vast buckle for his widow's gown:
Her infant grandame's whistle next it grew,
The bells she jingled, and the whistle blew;
95 Then in a bodkin graced her mother's hairs,
Which long she wore, and now Belinda wears.)
"Boast not my fall," he cried, "insulting foe!
Thou by some other shalt be laid as low.
Nor think to die dejects my lofty mind:
100 All that I dread is leaving you behind!

Rather than so, ah, let me still survive,
And burn in Cupid's flames—but burn alive."
"Restore the Lock!" she cries; and all around
"Restore the Lock!" the vaulted roofs rebound.
105  Not fierce Othello in so loud a strain
Roared for the handkerchief that caused his pain.
But see how oft ambitious aims are crossed,
And chiefs contend till all the prize is lost!
The lock, obtained with guilt, and kept with pain,
110  In every place is sought, but sought in vain:
With such a prize no mortal must be blessed,
So Heaven decrees! with Heaven who can contest?
    Some thought it mounted to the lunar sphere,
Since all things lost on earth are treasured there.
115  There heroes' wits are kept in ponderous vases,
And beaux' in snuffboxes and tweezer cases.
There broken vows and deathbed alms are found,
And lovers' hearts with ends of riband bound,
The courtier's promises, and sick man's prayers,
120  The smiles of harlots, and the tears of heirs,
Cages for gnats, and chains to yoke a flea,
Dried butterflies, and tomes of casuistry.
    But trust the Muse—she saw it upward rise,
Though marked by none but quick, poetic eyes
125  (So Rome's great founder to the heavens         *Romulus was borne to heaven in a storm-cloud*
      withdrew,°                                     *and later deified.*
To Proculus alone confessed in view);
A sudden star, it shot through liquid° air,          *Clear.*
And drew behind a radiant trail of hair.
Not Berenice's locks first rose so bright,°          *The hair which the*
130  The heavens bespangling with disheveled           *Egyptian queen*
      light.                                          *Berenice dedicated to*
The Sylphs behold it kindling as it flies,           *the gods to insure her*
And pleased pursue its progress through              *husband's safe return*
      the skies.                                      *from war was turned*
    This the beau monde shall from the                *into a constellation.*
      Mall° survey,                                   *A walkway in St.*
And hail with music its propitious ray.               *James's Park*
135  This the blest lover shall for Venus take,
And send up vows from Rosamonda's Lake.°              *A small lake in*
This Partridge° soon shall view in cloudless          *St. James's Park.*
      skies,                                          *An astrologer who*
When next he looks through Galileo's       *made foolish predictions.*
      eyes;°                                          *A telescope*

And hence the egregious wizard shall foredoom
140 The fate of Louis, and the fall of Rome.
    Then cease, bright nymph! to mourn thy ravished hair,
Which adds new glory to the shining sphere!
Not all the tresses that fair head can boast,
Shall draw such envy as the Lock you lost.
145 For, after all the murders of your eye,
When, after millions slain, yourself shall die:
When those fair suns shall set, as set they must,
And all those tresses shall be laid in dust,
This Lock the Muse shall consecrate to fame,
150 And 'midst the stars inscribe Belinda's name.

# Appendix

# What to Say About a Poem*

## WILLIAM K. WIMSATT

What to say about a poem. How to say something special about a poem, different from what is said by the ordinary reader, different quite likely from what would be said by the poet himself. Our professional preoccupation as teachers, scholars, critics, sometimes conceals from us the fact that our kind of interest in poems is after all a very special thing—a vocational or shop interest, somewhat strained perhaps at moments, even somewhat uncouth. Poems, a cultivated person might suppose, are made to be read and enjoyed. If I read a poem and enjoy it, why should I then proceed to dwell on it as an object about which something deliberate and elaborate has to be *said*—unless in a surreptitious effort to borrow or emulate some of the self-expression enjoyed by the poet? What a critic or a teacher does with a poem is not, certainly, the main thing the poem is intended for or fit for. The poem is not the special property of these professionals. What they do with it in any deeper sense, what their purpose and methods are, we had better not try to say too quickly. It is the problem of this essay.

## II

Many centuries of literary theory have equipped us with a large array of now more or less standard topics, handles or labels, for the analysis of poems. We are disciplined to speak of the *theme* (the most abstractive and assertive kind of meaning which the poem has), and we wish to distinguish this from its realization or more concrete definition in various expressive features conceived as denser, more real, than theme, and yet translucent with meaning. We speak of *diction, imagery, metaphor, symbol* (above all symbol); we sometimes resurrect such older terms as *personification, allegory, fable*. And in our most ambitious, or in our vaguer and more portentous, moments, we sum up such terms and magnify them into the name of *myth*. At the same time, we speak of the movement of the poem in time, its *rhythm*, and more

* From *Hateful Contraries* by William K. Wimsatt, Copyright 1965 by the University of Kentucky Press. Reprinted by permission of the publishers, the University of Kentucky Press, and the author. [Footnotes omitted—Ed.]

precisely its *meter*, its *lines*, *stanzas*, *rhymes*, *alliteration* and *assonance*, its echoes, turns, agnominations, and puns, and also the more directly imitative qualities of its sound, the *onomatopoeia*, representative meter, and sound symbolism, the orchestration, and all that. Sound tangles with meaning. A whole poem has a *pattern*, both of meaning and of sound, interacting. It is an act of speech and hence a *dramatization* of a meaning; it is set in a landscape or a decor, an *atmosphere*, a world, a place full of flora and fauna, constellations, furniture, accoutrements, all "symbolic" of course. It is spoken by some person, fictitious, or fictive, if we rightly conceive him, a *persona*, a mask, a mouthpiece, and hence it has a point of view and a variety of emotive endowments, an attitude toward its materials, and toward the speaker himself, a self-consciousness, and a *tone* of voice towards you and me the readers or *audience*. And often we too, if we rightly conceive ourselves, are a part of the fiction of the poem. Or at least we read only over the shoulder of some person or group that is the immediate and fictive audience. The poem is furthermore (especially if we are historical critics) a poem of a certain type or *genre* (tragic, comic, epic, elegiac, satiric, or the like), and this conception implies certain *rules*, a tradition, a decorum, convention, or expectancy. The genre and its aspects are in truth a part of the language of the sophisticated poet, a backdrop for his gestures, a sounding board against which he plays off his effects. Often enough, or perhaps always, the exquisite poem presents a sort of finely blended or dramatically structured opposition of attitudes and of the meanings which lie behind them—their *objective correlatives*. Hence the poem has *tension* (stress and distress), it lives in conflict; its materials are warped, its diction strained, dislocated. Catachresis is only normal. That is to say, the poem is *metaphoric*. The metaphoric quality of the meaning turns out to be the inevitable counterpart of the mixed feelings. Sometimes this situation is so far developed as to merit the name of *paradoxical*, *ambiguous*, *ironic*. The poem is subtle, elusive, tough, *witty*. Always it is an indirect stratagem of its finest or deepest meaning.

I have been running over some of the main terms of our inherited grammar of criticism and attempting just a hint at some of their relationships—the pattern, if not of the poem, at least of criticism itself. I hope it is evident that I am in no sense unfriendly to this grammar of criticism or to any one of the terms of which it is composed. I am all in favor of a grammar of criticism and of our making it as sober, tight, accurate, and technically useful as may be possible. The grammar, for instance, must be especially firm in the areas of syntax and prosody, where the poet himself has, at various times in various languages and poetic traditions, been compelled to be, or has allowed himself to be, most tight and technical. It is important, for instance, to know that *Paradise Lost* is written in iambic pentameter, and if we let ourselves be pushed around at the whim of random musical or linguistic theory into finding three, four or seven or eight metrical beats in a Miltonic line of blank verse, we are making sad nonsense of literary history and of what this particular poet did and said. An analogous difficulty would be the enterprise of talking about the poet John Donne without the use of any such terms at all as paradox, metaphysical wit, irony.

On the other hand, grammar is grammar. And I will confess to a decided opinion that the kind of technical and quasi-technical matters which I have been naming ought to be discussed mainly at the level of generalization—they ought to be taken mainly as the preliminaries, the tuning-up exercises, the calisthenics of criticism. An essay on the theme of metaphor, of symbol, of lyrical dramatics, of irony, of meter, of rhyme or pun, is one sort of thing—it is likely to be extremely interesting and useful. But an interpretation or appreciation of a specific poem by the means mainly of an appeal to categories expressed by such terms is another sort of thing—this is likely in my opinion to be somewhat less interesting.

The purpose of any poem cannot be simply to be a work of art, to be artificial, or to embody devices of art. A critic or appreciator of a poem ought scarcely to be conceived as a person who has a commitment to go into the poem and bring out trophies under any of the grammatical heads, or to locate and award credits for such technicalities—for symbols, for ironies, for meter. These and similar terms will likely enough be useful in the course of the critic's going into and coming out of a given poem. But that is a different thing. To draw a crude analogy: It would be an awkward procedure to introduce one human being to another (one of our friends to another) with allusions to commonplaces of his anatomy, or labels of his race, creed, or type of neurosis. The analogy, as I have said, is crude. Poems are not persons. Still there may be a resemblance here sufficient to give us ground for reflection.

I am supposing that the specific thing we are discussing is what to say about a given poem—rather than how to make a survey of poetry in general in order to write a grammar of poetry. Not the most precisely definable and graded features of poems in general, the accepted grammar, but something in a sense even more generic, the basic activity of our own minds by which we examine a given individual poem—this is what I now wish to talk for a while about. This activity of our own in examining a poem, let me add immediately and firmly, does suppose that an object, with definable features, is there, independent of us, for us to examine.

### III

Let us, for one thing, remember, and observe in passing, that as teachers, for instance, we are likely to put ourselves in a Socratic relation to our pupils—setting them exercises, asking them questions. So that our own first question, what to *say* about a poem, is likely enough to assume the shape: what to *ask* about a poem. This I think is a very special, intrinsic and difficult aspect of our professional problem. If we assume that we do know, roughly, the correct things to say about a poem, how can these be transposed into good questions? Sometimes the very attempt will reveal the emptiness of what we thought we had to say. This question about questions is obviously a matter of art and tact, our own personality and that of our pupils, and I believe that nobody ought to presume to write any manuals about it. But let me stay long enough to suggest that a good question about a poem should have at least two qualities—it should stand in a middle ground between two kinds of fault. That is, in the first place, it should have in mind an answer that is better than arbitrary or prescriptive. It should not mean in effect merely: "Guess what I am thinking about. Or, tell me what I ought to be thinking about." "How does the imagery, or the meter, in this poem accomplish its purpose?" We may look on such a question, if we like, as setting an exercise, a way of eliciting or demanding an overnight paper. It is scarcely a part of a Socratic discussion. But then in the second place, the question ought not to be so good that it betrays or implies its own answer or the terms of its answer. "Is the imagery of the dead trees in this poem well suited to express the idea of mortality?" The answer that is being angled for ought to be more than simply *yes* or *no*—unless perhaps as a mere preliminary to some further and more real question. Sometimes, oddly enough, the two faults of question-making turn out to be the same thing—or at least some of our more careless questions will invite being taken in either of two ways, both empty. Rather accurate parodies of the world of discourse we teachers are capable of creating appear sometimes in the jokes, gags, or riddles (learned I suppose mostly over breakfast radio) which become the favorites of our youngest pupils. "What is large and red and eats rocks?" A certain father tried to be the ingenious pupil and answered, "A large poem by William Blake." But that of course was wrong. The answer was: "A large red rock-eater." A good question should have a definite answer—different from the question and yet entailed by it. Some questions the teacher will ask mainly for the sake of giving himself the occasion for reciting the answer. (I do not say that is always bad.) A good question about a poem will be less like the example I have already given than like this other from the same source—though not exactly like this either. "What is the difference between a lead pipe and an infatuated Dutchman?" The father, though a teacher of poetry, gave up. The answer of course is that one is a hollow cylinder, the other is a silly Hollander.

## IV

At the outset what can we be sure of? Mainly that a person says or means something, or ought to mean something (or ought to if we as teachers have any business with it—perhaps that is the safe minimum). The meaning of the poem may be quite obscure and difficult (rough, opaque and resistant to first glance), or it may be smooth and easy, perhaps deceptively smooth and easy, a nice surface and seemingly transparent. For either kind of poem, the simplest, but not the least important, kind of observation we can make, the simplest question we can ask, is the kind which relates to the dictionary. What does a certain word or phrase mean? We are lucky enough, I am assuming, to have a poem which contains some archaic, technical, or esoteric expression, which the class, without previous research, will not understand. If we are even luckier, the word has another, a modern, an easy and plausible meaning, which conceals the more difficult meaning. (Ambiguity, double or simultaneous meaning, our grammar instructs us, is a normal situation in poems.) In any case, we can put our question in two stages: "Are there any difficulties or questions with this stanza?" "Well, in that case, Miss Proudfit, what does the word *braw* mean?" "What does *kirkward* mean?" "When six braw gentlemen kirkward shall carry ye." We are lucky, I say, not simply that we have a chance to teach the class something—to earn our salary in a clear and measurable way. But of course because we hereby succeed in turning the attention of the class to the poem, to the surface, and then through the surface. They may begin to suspect the whole of this surface. They may ask a few questions of their own. This is success. A person who has been a teacher for a number of years masters the problem of knowing his lesson only to experience the more difficult problem of trying to remember what it is like not to know it.

V

The answers to the kind of questions we have just noticed lie in a clean, dictionary region of meaning. This kind of meaning is definitely, definably, and provably there—some of our pupils just did not happen to be aware of it. Let us call this *explicit* meaning. I believe it is important to give this kind of meaning a name and to keep it fixed. The act of expounding this meaning also needs a name. Let us call it *explanation*—explanation of the explicit.

Obviously, our talking about the poem will not go far at this level—not much farther than our translation of Caesar or Virgil in a Latin reading class.

And so we proceed, or most often we do, to another level of commentary on the poem—not necessarily second *in order* for every teacher or for every poem, but at least early and fundamental, or in part so. This level of commentary may usefully be called *description* of a poem—not explanation, just description. There is no way of describing the weather report, except to repeat what it says—describing the weather. A poem, on the other hand, not only says something, but *is* something. "A poem," we know, "should not mean but be." And so the poem itself especially invites description.

The meter of a poem, for instance, is of certain kind, with certain kinds of variations and certain relations to the syntax; one kind of word rhymes with another kind (*Aristotle* with *bottle*, in Byron; *Adam* with *madam*, in Yeats); some conspicuous repetition or refrain in a poem shows partial variations ("On the Ecchoing Green. . . . On the darkening Green." "Could frame thy fearful symmetry. . . . Dare frame thy fearful symmetry"). Some unusual word is repeated several times in a short poem, or a word appears in some curious position. Some image (or "symbol") or cluster of images recurs in a tragedy or is played against some other image or cluster. Shakespeare's *Hamlet*, for instance, may be described as a dramatic poem which concerns the murder of a father and a son's burden of exacting revenge. At the same time it is a work which exhibits a remarkable number and variety of images relating to the expressive arts and to the criticism of the arts—music, poetry, the theater. "That's an ill phrase, a vile phrase; 'beautified' is a vile phrase." "Speak the speech, I pray you . . . trippingly on the tongue." "Govern these ventages with your finger and thumb . . . it will discourse most eloquent music."

Description in the most direct sense moves inside the poem, accenting the parts and showing their relations. It may also, however, look outside the poem. *Internal* and *external* are complementary. The external includes all the kinds of history in which the poem has its setting. A specially important kind of history, for example, is the literary tradition itself. The small neat squared-off quatrains of Andrew Marvell's *Horatian Ode* upon Oliver Cromwell go in a very exact way with the title and with the main statement of the poem. Both in ostensible theme and in prosody the poem is a kind of echo of Horatian alcaics in honor of Caesar Augustus. The blank verse of Milton's *Paradise Lost* and the couplets of Dryden's translation of the *Aeneid* are both attempts to find an equivalent for, or a vehicle of reference to, the hexameters of Greek and Latin epic poetry. A poem in William Blake's *Songs of Innocence* is written in simple quatrains, four rising feet or three to a line, with perhaps alternate rhymes. These are something like the stanzas of a folk ballad, but they are more like something else. A more immediate antecedent both of Blake's metric and of his vocabulary of childlike piety, virtues and vices, hopes and fears, is the popular religious poetry of the eighteenth century, the hymns sung at the evangelical chapels, written for children by authors like Isaac Watts or Christopher Smart.

## VI

We can insist, then, on *description* of poems, both *internal* and *external*, as a moment of critical discourse which has its own identity and may be usefully recognized and defined. Let us hasten to add, however, that in making the effort to define this moment we are mainly concerned with setting up a platform for the accurate construction of something further.

The truth is that description of a poetic structure is never simply a report on appearances (as it might be, for instance, if the object were a painted wooden box). Description of a poetic structure is inevitably also an engagement with *meanings* which inhere in that structure. It is a necessary first part of the engagement with certain kinds of meaning. (*Certain kinds*—in the long run we shall want to lay some emphasis on that qualification. But for the moment the point is that there is meaning.) In the critic's discourse "pure description" will always have a hard time taking the "place of sense."

Perhaps we shall feel guilty of stretching the meaning of the word *meaning* slightly, but unless we are willing to leave many kinds of intimation out of our account of poetry, we shall have to say, for example, that Byron meant that criticism had fallen on evil days—and that it didn't matter very much. "Longinus o'er a bottle, Or, Every Poet his *own* Aristotle." We shall have to say, surely we shall wish to say, that Milton in the opening of his *Paradise Lost* means, "This is the language and style of epic, the greatest kind of poetry; and this is the one theme that surpasses those of the greatest epics of antiquity." ("This"—in a sense—"is an epic to end all epics." As it did.) Alexander Pope in his *Epistle to Augustus* means, "This is a poem to the King of England which sounds curiously like the Epistle of Horace to the Emperor Augustus. Let anybody who cares or dares notice how curious it sounds." Shakespeare means that the action of *Hamlet* takes place on a stage, in a world, where relations between appearance and reality are manifold and some of them oddly warped.

Through description of poems, then, we move back to meaning —though scarcely to the same kind of meaning as that with which we were engaged in our initial and simple explanation of words. Through description, we arrive at a kind of meaning which ought to have its own special name. We can safely and usefully, I think, give it the simple name of the *implicit*. What we are doing with it had better too be given a special name. Perhaps *explication* is the best, though the harsher word *explicitation* may seem invited. The realms of the explicit and the implicit do not, of course, constitute sealed-off separate compartments. Still there will be some meanings which we can say are clearly explicit, and some which are clearly but implicit.

I believe that we ought to work to keep ourselves keenly aware of two things concerning the nature of implicit meaning. One of these is the strongly directive and selective power of such meaning—the power of the *pattern*, of the main formally controlling purpose in the well-written poem (in terms of Gestalt psychology, the principle of "closure"). It is this which is the altogether sufficient and compelling reason in many of our decisions about details of meaning which we proceed, during our discussion of the poem, to make quite explicit—though the dictionary cannot instruct us. In the third stanza of Marvell's *Garden*: "No white or red was ever seen / So am'rous as this lovely green." How do we know that the words *white* and *red* refer to the complexions of the British ladies?—and not, for instance, to white and red roses? The word *am'rous* gives a clue. The whole implicit pattern of meaning in the poem proves it. In these lines of this poem the words can mean nothing else. In Marvell's *Ode* on Cromwell: ". . . now the *Irish* are asham'd to see themselves in one Year tam'd. . . . They can affirm his Praises best, And have, though overcome, confest How good he is, how just, And fit for highest Trust." How do we show that these words do not express simply a complacent English report, for the year 1650, on the ruthless efficiency of Cromwell in Ireland? Only by appealing to the delicately managed intimations of the whole poem. The cruder reading, which might be unavoidable in some other context, will here reveal (in the interest of a supposedly stolid historical accuracy) a strange critical indifference to the extraordinary finesse of Marvell's poetic achievement. "Proud Maisie is in the wood, Walking so early. . . . 'Tell me, thou bonny bird, When shall I marry me?'—'When six braw gentlemen Kirkward shall carry ye.'" How do we know, how do we prove to our freshman class, that the word *proud* does not mean in the first place—does not necessarily mean at all—conceited, unlikable, nasty, unlovable, that Maisie does not suffer a fate more or less well deserved (withered and grown old as a spinster—an example of poetic justice) ? Only, I think, by appealing to the whole contour and intent of this tiny but exquisitely complete poem.

> "Who makes the bridal bed,
>     Birdie, say truly?"—
> "The gray-headed sexton
>     That delves the grave duly.
>
> "The glow-worm o'er grave and stone
>     Shall light thee steady.
> The owl from the steeple sing,
>     'Welcome, proud lady.'"

The second thing concerning implicit meaning which I think we ought to stress is exactly its character as implicit—and this in reaction against certain confused modes of talk which sometimes prevail. It was a hard fight for criticism, at one time not so long past, to gain recognition of the formal and implicit at all as a kind of meaning. But that fight being in part won, perhaps a careless habit developed of talking about all sorts and levels of meaning as if they all were meaning in the same direct and simple way. And this has brought anguished bursts of protest from more sober and literal scholars. The critic seems all too gracefully and readily to move beyond mere explanation (being a sophisticated man, he feels perhaps the need to do relatively little of this). He soars or plunges into descriptions of the colors and structures of the poem, with immense involvements of meaning, manifold explicitations—yet all perhaps in one level tone of confident and precise insistence, which scarcely advertises or even admits what is actually going on. The trouble with this kind of criticism is that it knows too much. Students, who of course know too little, will sometimes render back and magnify this kind of weakness in weird parodies, innocent sabotage. "I am overtired / Of the great harvest I myself desired," proclaims the man who lives on the farm with the orchard, the cellar bin, the drinking trough, and the woodchuck, in Robert Frost's *After Apple-Picking*. "This man," says the student in his homework paper, "is tired of life. He wants to go to sleep and die." This we mark with a red pencil. Then we set to work, somehow, in class, to retrieve the "symbolism." This monodrama of a tired apple-picker, with the feel of the ladder rungs in his instep, bears nearly the same relation to the end of a country fair, the end of a victorious football season, of a long vacation, or of a full lifetime, as a doughnut bears to a Christmas wreath, a ferris wheel, or the rings of Saturn. *Nearly* the same relation, let us say. A poem is a kind of shape, a cunning and precise shape of words and human experience, which has something of the indeterminacy of a simpler physical shape, round or square, but which at the same time invites and justifies a very wide replication or reflection of itself in the field of our awareness.

> Till the little ones, weary
> No more can be merry;
> The sun does descend,
> And our sports have an end.
> Round the laps of their mothers
> Many sisters and brothers,
> Like birds in their nest,
> Are ready for rest,
> And sport no more seen
> On the darkening Green.

What experience has any member of the class ever had, or what experiences can he think of or imagine, that are parallel to or concentric to that of the apple-picker? of the Ecchoing Green? —yet the words of the poem do not *mean* these other experiences in the same way that they mean the apples, the ladder, the man, the sport and the green. The kind of student interpretation which I have mentioned may be described as the fallacy of the literal feedback. Proud Maisie translated into conceited Maisie may be viewed as a miniature instance of the same. And this will illustrate the close relation between the two errors of implicit reading which I have just been trying to describe. The uncontrolled reading is very often the over-explicit reading.

## VII

Explanation, then—of the explicit and clearly ascertainable but perhaps obscure or disguised meanings of words; description—of the poem's structure and parts, its shape and colors, and its historical relations; explication—the turning of such description as far as possible into meaning. These I believe are the teacher-critic's staple commitments—which we may sum up, if we wish, in some such generic term as *elucidation* or *interpretation*.

It is difficult to illustrate these matters evenly from any single short poem. Let me, nevertheless, make the effort. Not to show the originality of my own critical judgment, but to keep within the area of what is readily available and plausible, I choose the four quatrains of William Blake's *London* in his *Songs of Experience*.

I wander thro' each charter'd street
Near where the charter'd Thames does flow,
And mark in every face I meet
Marks of weakness, marks of woe.

In every cry of every Man,
In every infant's cry of fear,
In every voice, in every ban,
The mind-forg'd manacles I hear.

How the Chimney-sweeper's cry
Every black'ning Church Appalls;
And the hapless Soldier's sigh
Runs in blood down Palace walls.

But most thro' midnight streets I hear
How the youthful Harlot's curse
Blasts the new born Infant's tear,
And blights with plagues the Marriage hearse.

Let me remark briefly that Blake engraved and printed and illuminated this poem as part of a pictorially designed page. But I believe that this poem (if perhaps not all of Blake's similarly illustrated poems) can be fully understood without any picture.

A further special remark is required by the fact that an early draft of this poem, which is available in Blake's notebook, the celebrated Rossetti manuscript, gives us several variant readings, even variants of key words in the poem. Such avenues of access to the poet's process of composition, a favorite kind of resort for the biographical detective, may also I believe be legitimately enough invoked by a teacher as an aid to exposition. Surely the variant reading, the fumbled and rejected inspiration, makes a convenient enough focus on the actual reading. We suppose that the poet did improve his composition, and usually he did. So if word A is worse, *why* is word B better, or best? Comparison opens inquiry, promotes realization. Sometimes the discovery of such an unravelled thread, in our learned edition of the poet, will save a classroom discussion which was otherwise moving toward vacuity. Nevertheless I choose here not to invoke the interesting variants to Blake's poem, because I believe the existence and the exhibition of such genetic vestiges is not intrinsic to the confrontation of our minds with the poem. Not that to invoke the variants would be unfair—it is simply unnecessary. If we really need inferior variants, we can make up some of our own. And perhaps we ought to.

Perhaps there is no single word in this poem which calls for the simple dictionary work which I have defined as the level of mere explanation. But the word *charter'd*, used twice in the first two lines, is nearly such a word. At any rate, its emphatic and reiterated assertion, its somewhat curious ring in its context, as well as its position at the start of the poem, make it a likely word to begin with. How is a street chartered? How is the Thames chartered? A charter is a written document, delivered by a governmental authority and granting privileges, recognizing rights, or creating corporate entities, boroughs, universities, trading companies, utilities. It is privilege, immunity, publicly conceded right. The Great Charter (*Magna Charta*) is a glorious instance of the concept in the history of men who speak English. I have been following, where it led me, the article under the word *Charter* in the *Oxford English Dictionary on Historical Principles*. But surely the great Dictionary is mistaken when under meaning 3.2 *figurative*. "Privileged, licensed," it quotes Shakespeare's *Henry the Fifth*, "When he speaks, The Ayre, a Charter'd Libertine, is still," and shortly after that, Blake, *Songs of Experience*, "Near where the charter'd Thames does flow." Surely the eminent Victorian person who compiled that entry was little given to the modern critical sin of looking for ironies in poetry. The force of that reiterated word in the first two lines of Blake's poem must have something to do with a tendency of the word, in the right context (and Blake's poem is that context), to mean nearly the opposite of those meanings of advantage listed in the Dictionary. For chartered privilege is a legalistic thing, which sounds less good when we call it vested interest, and which entails an inevitable obverse, that is, restriction or restraint. How indeed could the street or the river be chartered in any of the liberating senses listed in the Dictionary? It is the traffic on them or the right to build houses along them that is chartered in the sense of being conceded—to somebody. And this inevitably means that for somebody else—probably for you and me—the privilege is the restriction. Thus the strange twisted aptness, the happy catachresis, of the wanderer's calling so mobile and natural a force as the river chartered at all. The fact is that this meaning of the word *chartered* is not listed in the *Oxford Dictionary*.

We began with the Dictionary, but we have had to go beyond it, to correct it in a specific point, and even to reverse its general drift. Examples of dictionary explanation of words in poems almost always turn out to be not quite pure.

To turn away from the attempt at such explanation, then— what opportunities do we find for simply *describing* this poem —and first, with regard to its immediate historical contexts? Perhaps some note on the chimney sweeper will be needed for our twentieth-century American pupils. We can look a little to one side and see Blake's angry poem *The Chimney Sweeper* in the *Songs of Experience*: "A little black thing among the snow, Crying 'weep!' 'weep!' in notes of woe!" We can look back and see the companion *Chimney Sweeper*, tenderly comical, poignant, in the *Songs of Innocence*. ". . . I said 'Hush, Tom! never mind it, for when your head's bare You know that the soot cannot spoil your white hair.'" An Act of Parliament of 1788 had attempted to prohibit the employment of chimney sweeps until they were eight years old. In winter they began work at 7 a.m., in summer at 5. Their heads were shaved to reduce the risk of their hair catching fire from pockets of smouldering soot. An essay on the eighteenth-century London practice of chimney-sweeping would of course be an explication, *in extenso*, of the third stanza of this poem. We could add notes too for this stanza on the wars and armies of the period, on the condition of the London churches (the blackening of Portland limestone outside—suppositions about the failure of the ministry inside, priestly symbols of oppression in other lyrics by Blake), or for the fourth stanza we could investigate harlots in eighteenth-century London. But I believe it is part of the power of this particular poem that it scarcely requires any very elaborate descriptive explications of this sort. "We can do pretty well with the poem," says one commentator, "in contexts of our own manufacture or out of our own experience."

Another external point of reference, a part of Blake's immediate literary and religious tradition, has already been named—that is, when we alluded to the simple metrics and the innocent language of the eighteenth-century evangelical hymns. Blake's *Songs of Innocence and of Experience*, says one critic, are "almost a parody" of such popular earlier collections as the *Divine Songs Attempted in Easy Language for the Use of Children* by the nonconformist minister and logician Isaac Watts. Blake knew that collection well. And thus, a certain *Song* entitled *Praise for Mercies Spiritual and Temporal*.

> Whene'er I take my walks abroad,
>   How many poor I see;
> What shall I render to my God
>   For all his gifts to me.
>
> . . . . . . . . . . . . .
>
> How many children in the street,
>   Half naked I behold!
> While I am cloth'd from head to feet,
>   And cover'd from the cold.

The echoes of such socially innocent hymnology in the minds and ears of Blake and his generation make, as I have suggested, a part of the meaning of his vocabulary and rhythm, part of a historic London sounding board, against which we too can enjoy a more resonant reading of the bitterness and irony of the wanderer in the chartered streets.

But to turn back to the words of our poem and to inquire whether any *internal* features of it deserve descriptive notice: For one thing, I should want a class to notice how the simple hymn-like stanzas of this poem are fortified or specialized in a remarkable way by a kind of phonemic tune, or prominent and stark, almost harsh, succession of similar emphatic syllables. This tune is announced in the opening verb *wander*, then immediately picked up and reiterated, doubly and triply: *chartered* street, *chartered Thames*, "And *mark* in every face . . . *Marks* of Weakness, *marks* of woe." The word *mark* indeed, the inner mental act, the outer graven sign, is the very motif of this marking repetition. It was more than a semantic or dictionary triumph when Blake revising his poem hit on the word *chartered*—rejecting the other quite different-sounding word which we need not mention, which appears in the Rossetti manuscript.

The student of the poem will easily pick out the modulations of the theme through the rest of the poem: the rhyme words *man* and *ban*, the emphatic syllable of *ma*nacles, the *black*'ning Church, the *hap*less sigh, the *Palace Walls* . . . *Har*lot, *Blasts*, and *Mar*riage. But what is the meaning of this phonetic pattern? A certain meaning, not in the sense necessarily of what Blake fully intended or would have confessed or defined if we had asked him, but in the sense of something which is actually conveyed if we will let it be conveyed, has been pretty much implied in the very description of the pattern. According to our temperaments and our experiences, and as our imagination is more auditory, eidetic, or kinesthetic, we will realize the force of this phonetic marking in images of insistently wandering, tramping feet, in a savage motion of the arms and head, in a bitter chanting, a dark repetition of indictments. Any one of these images, as I attempt to verbalize it, is perhaps excessive; no one is specifically necessary. But all of these and others are relevant.

We have said that the word *chartered* when applied to the street and even more when applied to the river is an anomaly. A close inspection of this poem will reveal a good many curiosities in its diction. Notice, for example, the word *cry*, which occurs three times in the course of stanzas two and three. Why do men cry in the streets of London? In addition to various random cries of confusion, hurry, and violence (which we are surely entitled to include in the meaning of the word), there is the more special and more continuous London street *cry*, the "proclamation," as the Dictionary has it, of wares or of services. If we had plenty of time for history we could read Addison's *Spectator* on "Street Cries." A more immediately critical interest is served when we notice that the steadily clamorous background of the London scene of charter and barter merges by a kind of metaphoric glide, in the next two lines, into a medley of other vocal sounds, "cries," in another sense, of fear, "voices," "bans"—that is to say, legal or official yells, proclamations, summonses, prohibitions, curses. Are the kinds of cries really separate, or are all much the same? In the next line the infant cry of fear merges literally with the cry of service—"sweep, sweep," or "weep, weep," as we learn the pronunciation from Blake's two Chimney Sweeper songs. The whole poem proceeds not only by pregnant repetitions but by a series of extraordinary conjunctions and compressions, by a pervasive emergence of metaphoric intimation from the literal details of the Hogarthian scene. Consider, for instance, how to *appall* is to dismay or terrify, and etymologically perhaps to make *pale*. Doubtless the syntax says here in the first place that the unconsciously accusing cry of the infant sweep strikes dismay, even a kind of pallor, into these irrelevant, mouldering, and darkening fabrics. At the same time the syntax does not forbid a hint of the complementary sense that the walls throw back the infant cry in ineffectual and appalled echoes. The strange assault of pitiful sounds upon the very color of the walls, which is managed in these first two lines by verbal intimation, erupts in the next two beyond verbalism into the bold, surrealistically asserted vision of the *sigh* which attaches itself as blood to palace walls.

> But most thro' midnight streets I hear
> How the youthful Harlot's curse
> Blasts the new born Infant's tear,
> And blights with plagues the Marriage hearse.

The devotee of Blake may, by consulting the Rossetti manuscript, discover that the poet took extraordinary pains with this last stanza of the poem (which was an afterthought): he wrote it and rewrote it deleting words and squeezing alternatives onto his already used-up page. Clearly he intended that a lot of meaning should inhere in this densely contrived stanza—the climax, the *most* appalling instance, of the assault of the city sounds upon the citadels, the institutions, the persons of the chartered privilege. The new role of the infant in this stanza, lying between the harlot and the major target of her curse, and the impatient energy, the crowding of sense, from the harlot and her curse, through the blight, the plague, to the ghastly paradox of that final union of words—the marriage hearse—perhaps we had better leave this to a paper by our students, rather than attempt to exhaust the meaning in class.

I have perhaps already said too much about this one short poem. Yet I have certainly not said all that might be said. Relentless criticism of a poem, the technique of the lemon-squeezer, is not to my mind an ideal pedagogic procedure. It is not even a possibility. A descriptive explication of a poem is both more and less than a multiple and exhaustive précis. Our aim I think should be to say certain selected, intelligible things about a poem, enough to establish the main lines of its technical achievement, of its symbolic shape. When we have done that much, we understand the poem—even if there are grace notes and overtones which have escaped our conscious notice.

## VIII

Let me back off then from the poem by William Blake and return once more, briefly, to my main argument. *Explanation*, *description*, and *explication*: we can recognize three phases of our interpretation of the poem, though they prove to be more closely entangled and merged with one another than we might have realized at the beginning. But are they all? Is there not another activity which has been going on in our minds, almost inevitably, all this while? The activity of *appreciation*. All this time, while reading the poem so carefully, have we not also been liking it or disliking it? Admiring it or despising it? Presumably we have. And presumably we ought now to ask ourselves this further question: Is there any connection between the things we have managed so far to say about the poem and the kind of response we experience toward it? Our liking it or our disliking it? Are we inclined to try to explain why we like the poem? Do we know how to do this? More precisely: Would a statement of our liking the poem, an act of praise or appreciation, be something different from (even though perhaps dependent upon) the things we have already been saying? Or has the appreciation already been sufficiently implied or entailed by what we have been saying?

At the first level, that of simple dictionary explanation, very little, we will probably say, has been implied. And very little, we will most likely say, in many of our motions at the second level, the simply descriptive. It is not a merit in a poem, or surely not much of a merit, that it should contain any given vocabulary, say of striking or unusual words, or even that it should have metaphors, or that it should have meter or any certain kind of meter, or rhymes, as any of these entities may be purely conceived.

But that—as we have been seeing—is to put these matters of simple explanation and simple description more simply and more abstractly than they are really susceptible of being put. We pass imperceptibly and quickly beyond these matters. We are inevitably and soon caught up in the demands of explication—the realization of the vastly more rich and interesting implicit kinds of meaning. We are engaged with features of a poem which—given always other features too of the whole context—do tend to assert themselves as reasons for our pleasure in the poem and our admiration for it. We begin to talk about patterns of meaning; we encounter structures or forms which are radiant or resonant with meaning. Patterns and structures involve coherence (unity, coherence, and emphasis), and coherence is an aspect of truth and significance. I do not think that our evaluative intimations will often, if ever, advance to the firmness and completeness of a demonstration. Perhaps it is hardly conceivable that they should. But our discourse upon the poem will almost inevitably be charged with implications of its value. It will be more difficult to keep out these intimations than to let them in. Critics who have announced the most resolute programs of neutrality have found this out. Take care of the weight, the color, the shape of the poem, be fair to the explanation and description, the indisputable parts of the formal explication—the appreciation will be there, and it will be difficult to avoid having expressed it.

Explicatory criticism (or explicatory evaluation) is an account of a poem which exhibits the relation between its form and its meaning. Only poems which are worth something are susceptible of this kind of account. It is something like a definition of poetry to say that whereas rhetoric—in the sense of mere persuasion or sophistic—is a kind of discourse the power of which diminishes in proportion as the artifice of it is understood or seen through—poetry, on the other hand, is a kind of discourse the power of which—or the satisfaction which we derive from it—is actually increased by an increase in our understanding of the artifice. In poetry the artifice is art. This comes close I think to the center of the aesthetic fact.

## IX

One of the attempts at a standard of poetic value most often reiterated in past ages has been the doctrinal—the explicitly didactic. The aim of poetry, says the ancient Roman poet, is double, both to give pleasure and to teach some useful doctrine. You might get by with only one or the other, but it is much sounder to do both. Or, the aim of poetry is to teach some doctrine—and to do this convincingly and persuasively, by means of vividness and pleasure—as in effect the Elizabethan courtier and the eighteenth-century essayist would say. But in what does the pleasure consist? Why is the discourse pleasurable? Well, the aim of poetry is really to please us by means of or through the act of teaching us. The pleasure is a dramatized moral pleasure. Thus in effect some theories of drama in France during the seventeenth century. Or, the pleasure of poetry is a pleasure simply of tender and morally good feelings. Thus in effect the philosophers of the age of reason in England and France. And at length the date 1790 and Immanuel Kant's *Critique of Judgment*: which asserts that the end or effect of art is not teaching certainly, and not pleasure in anything like a simple sensuous way—rather it is something apart, a feeling, but precisely its own kind of feeling, the aesthetic. Art is autonomous—though related symbolically to the realm of moral values. Speaking from this nondidactic point of view, a critic ought to say, I should think, that the aesthetic merit of Blake's *London* does not come about because of the fact that London in that age witnessed evils which cried to Heaven for remedy, or because Blake was a Prophet Against Empire, or a Visionary Politician, or because at some time, perhaps a few years after he had written the poem, he may have come to view it as one article or moment in the development of an esoteric philosophy of imagination, a Fearful Symmetry of Vision, expanded gradually in allegorical glimpses during several phases of his life into a quasi-religious revelation or privilege which in some sense, at moments, he believed in. Blake's *London* is an achievement in words, a contained expression, a victory which resulted from some hours, or days, of artistic struggle, recorded by his pen on a page of the Rossetti manuscript.

Between the time of Immanuel Kant, however, and our own, some complications in the purity of the aesthetic view have developed. Through the romantic period and after, the poetic mind advanced pretty steadily in its own autonomous way, toward a claim to be in itself the creator of higher values—to be perhaps the only creator. Today there is nothing that the literary theorist—at least in the British- and American-speaking world—will be more eager to repudiate than any hint of moral or religious didacticism, any least intimation that the poem is to measure its meaning or get its sanction from any kind of authority more abstract or more overtly legislative than itself. But on the other hand there has probably never been a generation of teachers of literature less willing to admit any lack of high seriousness, of implicit and embodied ethical content, even of normative vision in the object of their study. Despite our reiterated denials of didacticism, we live in an age, we help to make an age, of momentous claims for poetry—claims the most momentous conceivable, as they advance more and more under the sanction of an absolutely creative and autonomous visionary imagination. The Visionary imagination perforce repudiates all but the tautological commitment to itself. And thus, especially when it assumes (as now it begins to do) the form of what is called the "Tragic Vision" (not "The Vision of Tragedy"), it is the newest version of the *Everlasting No*. Vision *per se* is the vision of itself. "Tragic Vision" is the nearly identical vision of "Absurdity." (War-weariness and war-horror, the developing mind and studies of a generation that came out of the second War and has been living in expectation of the third may go far to explain the phenomenon, but will not justify it.) Antidoctrine is of course no less a didactic energy than doctrine itself. It is the reverse of doctrine. No more than doctrine itself, can it be located or even approached by a discussion of the relation between poetic form and poetic meaning. Antidoctrine is actually asserted by the poems of several English romantic poets, and notably, it would appear, though it is difficult to be sure, by the "prophecies" of William Blake. The idea of it may be hence a part of these poems, though never their achieved result or expression. Any more than an acceptable statement of Christian doctrine is Milton's achieved expression in *Paradise Lost*, or a statement of Aristotelian ethics is the real business of Spenser's *Faerie Queene*. Today I believe no prizes are being given for even the best doctrinal interpretation of poems. (The homiletic or parabolic interpretation of Shakespeare, for example, has hard going with the reviewer.) On the other hand, if you are willing to take a hand in the exploitation of the neuroses, the misgivings, the anxieties, the infidelities of the age—if you have talents for the attitudes of Titanism, the graces needed by an impresario of the nuptials of Heaven and Hell, you are likely to find yourself in some sense rewarded. It is obvious I hope that I myself do not believe the reward will consist in the achievement of a valid account of the relation between poetic form and poetic meaning.

*Alphabetical List of Poets,*
*with Their Birth and Death Dates,*
*including Approximate Dates for*
*Anonymous Poems*

233